The M[illegible]
of t[illegible]
Hexhamshir[illegible] [illegible]scape

Greg Finch

HLHS
HEXHAM LOCAL HISTORY SOCIETY

Hexham Local History Society
Hexham, Northumberland
www.hexhamhistorian.org

First published 2022

ISBN: 978 0 9565078 8 4

Cover image: Burntshield Haugh, Graham Dixon
Back cover: Nubbock and Paise Common, c.1770. courtesy Allendale Estates

Contents

Preface and acknowledgements

This book has been long in the making. The foundations were researched and laid from the turn of the century as I started gathering material to study what actually lay behind the eye-catching label 'Medieval Village (site of)' on the Ordnance Survey map at Dotland. This and other research was drawn together for a talk in 2010. Since then a significant amount of documentary research, archaeological surveying, excavation, and heritage conservation work has added much more to our knowledge of the history of the place known locally as the Shire. Consequently I am indebted to many people who have helped me over the years, some of whom are sadly no longer with us. What follows is much the better for their generosity with time, thoughts, local knowledge and specialist expertise, or in granting access to their land. Where I have incorrectly interpreted their insights or drawn different conclusions I remain entirely responsible. My thanks go to Max Adams, Stewart Ainsworth, Penny Carter, Robin Charlton, Ailsa Dodds, Ian Forbes, Paul Frodsham, Trevor Golightly, Martin Green, Arthur and Stuart Hall, Ian Hancock, John Hetherington, Pete Lee, Hilary Kristensen, Andrew, David, and John Nixon, Edward Parker, Pat Pickworth, Stuart Proctor, Judith Reed, Albert Robinson, Peter Ryder, Fiona and Philip Scott, Davy Short, Liz Sobell, Mel and Judy Stobbs, Gill Whatmough, Anthony White, Derek White, and Brian Young. The staff of various record offices have been obliging and helpful along the way, particularly at Northumberland Archives, at the National Archives in Kew, and Durham University Library's Archives and Special Collections.

I am greatly obliged to Graham Dixon and Stefan Sobell who freely helped with providing high quality photographs, which they have allowed me to reproduce here. Full image credits are given at the rear of the book. Brian Robe took me on a flight in his light plane in stunningly clear winter weather in 2012, resulting in a number of the aerial views used here. The book has benefited enormously from the time given so generously by Steve and Sue Bland in working on its design, layout and print-setting. I am very grateful to them for this, as is the Hexham Local History Society's committee. Ian Hancock, Mark Runnacles Goodridge, James Smith and Liz Sobell from the Society's committee have been very helpful and supportive in seeing it through to publication. And, as ever, I am very grateful to my wife Julie for her patience and support over the long period during which the book has been in preparation.

Greg Finch, Hexhamshire, August 2022

Notes on the text

In order to avoid overburdening the largely narrative flow of the text, asides and notes are given only sparingly, where particular assertions depend on specific sources of information, and for direct quotations. Those who wish to follow them up will find these at the end of each chapter. A section on 'further reading' has been included at the end of the book which indicates the works which I have found most helpful, and which are recommended to those who wish to explore any of the topics covered in greater depth. Throughout the book maps are orientated with north at the top unless otherwise stated. Measurements are given in a combination of imperial and metric units on no consistent basis other than general familiarity. Thus heights are given in feet and metres, but distances typically in miles.

Abbreviations used

AA	*Archaeologia Aeliana*, annual journal of the Society of Antiquaries of Newcastle-upon-Tyne
AVH	S Ainsworth, Shedding Light on the North Pennines, The Allen Valleys and Hexhamshire Lidar Landscape Survey, (2016): unpublished report available from the Altogether Archaeology website at https://altogetherarchaeology.org/reports.php
Black Book	R Britnell, C Etty and A King (eds), *The Black Book of Hexham*, (2011)
DUL	Durham Univ Library Archives and Special Collections
HER	Historic Environment Record, a listing of sites in the landscape maintained by Northumberland County Council and available to search online at https://keystothepast.info/
HH	*Hexham Historian*, annual journal of the Hexham Local History Society
HN	A History of Northumberland
HN-3	Volume 3: A B Hinds, *Hexhamshire Part 1*, (1896)
HN-4	Volume 4: J C Hodgson, *Hexhamshire Part 2*, (1897)
HN-6	Volume 6: J C Hodgson, *Bywell St Peter, Bywell St Andrew, Slaley*, (1902)
NRO	Northumberland Archives at Woodhorn Colliery
OS	Ordnance Survey
TNA	The National Archives, Kew

Fig 1: Study Area – the Devil's Water valley

1. Introduction – the lie of the land

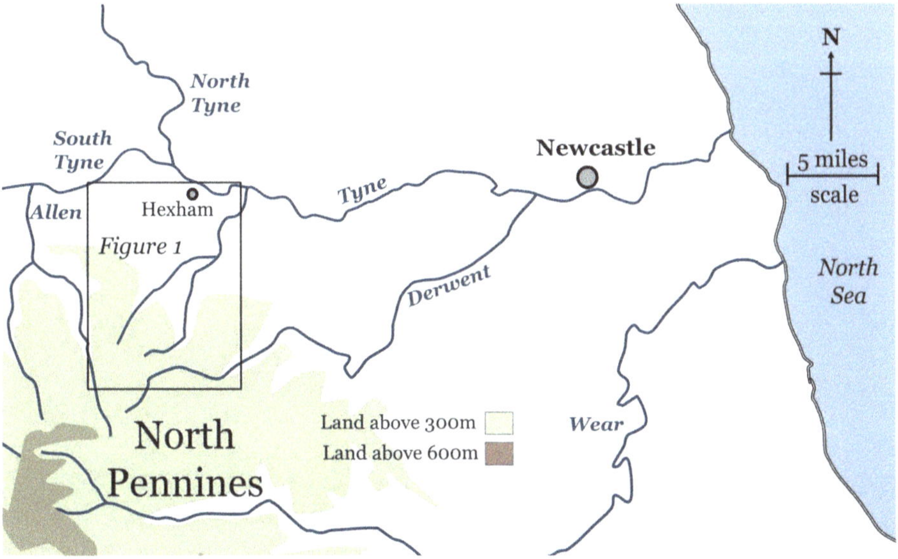

Fig 2: Hexhamshire in regional context

Hexhamshire

Hexhamshire lies in the south of Northumberland, one of the English counties covered by a volume in the series of landscape histories published in the wake of W G Hoskins' ground-breaking work *The Making of the English Landscape*. This new in-depth study of one small part of a northern border county is deliberately named after Hoskins' work, which has inspired an enormous body of research in more recent decades. It is intended mainly as an explanation (or an opinion at least) on how Hexhamshire has come to look as it does in the early 21st century, and the changes it has gone through along the way, at least so far as it is possible to identify them. Any attempt to describe what has already vanished, often many centuries ago, risks straying far into speculation, but it is important to try, for it helps to emphasise that what we see today is not a steady accumulation of features to reach some orderly finished state, but the latest snapshot of a landscape subject to the ebb and flow of change over millennia. The underlying themes of development and change through British history, which lie behind the subtle variations with which they played out in this particular corner of the country, are beyond the scope of this book, but suggestions for further reading are given at the end.

The map shown in Figure 1 might be helpful for those not familiar with the area, but it is also worth having an Ordnance Survey map to hand,

Fig 3 (top): North-eastwards towards Corbridge from Dotland
Fig 4 (above): Westwards along the Devil's Water valley below Long Lee

preferably the 1:25,000 Explorer map (OL 43), which shows field boundary detail. Wherever possible places referred to in the text can be found on the map, and grid references are given at relevant points in the index. The OS map is the essential guide to places that can be visited or viewed from access land, public highway, bridleway or footpath. Some landscape features mentioned in this study are on private land and therefore cannot be visited without the owner's permission.

The study's boundary is the catchment of the Devil's Water valley. It includes the slope running northwards to the Yarridge / racecourse road from the West Dipton Burn, the land east of the Devil's Water rising up to Corbridge Common, Slaley, Slaley Forest, Embley Fell and then roughly following the line of the Carriers' Way around Blackburn Head and the ridge north of Riddlehamhope. This is a natural physical unit, a small river basin surrounded by hills. It is about eight miles from the racecourse in the north to Harwoodshield Fell in the south, and about five and a half miles from Spital Shield's heather moorland in the west to Rye Hill & the Traveller's Rest pub, enclosing an area of about 26,500 acres (10,700 hectares), or 40 square miles ($104km^2$). This area is not quite the same as the current administrative boundary of Hexhamshire, but I nevertheless generally refer to 'the Shire' throughout, to use its local name. Whatever this loses in strict geographic accuracy, compared to 'the Devil's Water catchment area', it hopefully gains in brevity.

The lie of the land

Most of the Shire lies 500 feet (150 metres) or more above sea level, but this ranges from 200ft (60m) at Linnels Bridge up to 1,640ft (500m) south of Sinderhope Carrs just nine miles away to the south-west. These gradients illustrate the transition within this valley between upland and lowland Northumberland. The Shire lies where the North Pennines come down to Tynedale, running from west to east, a transition which adds interest to the landscape history of the area. It is a transition that can be seen quite clearly from the vantage point of Dotland. Look southwards and we see old woodland, newer plantations and shelter belts, fields and isolated farms in an upland dale below a mostly smooth horizon of heather moorland. In the summer it is a mellow patchwork of green and purple, but olive-grey, russet or sparkling white in winter's different moods. It is frequently windy, but alive in calmer summer weather with the sound of curlew, lapwing, skylark, buzzard, and distant plaintive sheep.

Look north and north-eastwards on the other hand and we see rolling mixed farmland, and more woodland, mostly older woodland in the valleys draining into the Devil's Water as it heads towards the Tyne Valley and Corbridge. Snokoe Hill stands out as a distinct landmark, often rising above early morning mist when it creeps up from the Tyne to mark out the course of the Devil's Water before being burned away by the rising sun. The orientation of the land itself, and the deep gorge of the West Dipton Burn running east-west, creating steep gradients into Hexham, begs the question why 'Shire' is not actually short for 'Corbridgeshire' rather than 'Hexhamshire', a point to return to later.

Local viewing points show a smoothly undulating land and mostly

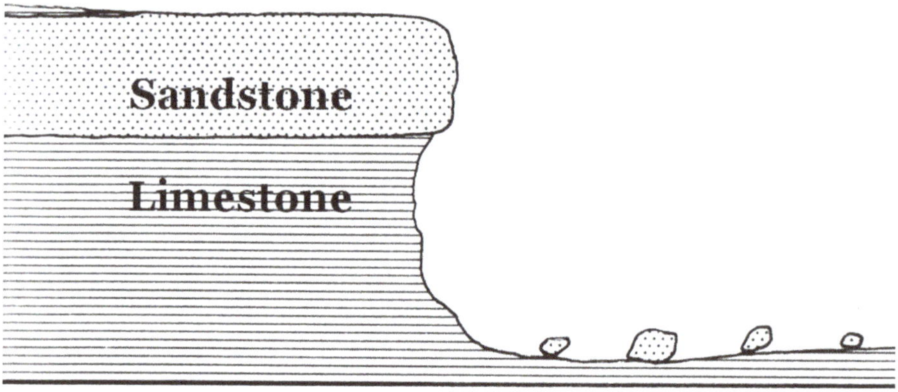

Figs 5 (top) and 6: Water action on sandstone and limestone in simple profile and on the Linn Burn upstream from Westburnhope

gentle slopes, quite different from the dramatic sweep of crags commanded by Hadrian's Wall, for example. In the Shire the drama is on a more intimate scale, hidden away in the deep valleys and gorges. The burns tumble over the rocks and refresh the senses, aided by the call of woodland birds, splashes of sunlight and bluebells and the heavy scent of wild garlic in May. It's these hidden valleys – westwards from the Dipton Mill pub for example, along the Rowley Burn below Whitley Mill, beside the Devil's Water upstream from Peth Foot below Ordley, or at Gingleshaugh and Hackford – that give a good idea of the underlying geology. This is vital to an understanding of the later history of the landscape.

Simplistically, the rocks that provide the Shire's physical foundation were mostly laid down 310 million years ago, in the Carboniferous period, and roughly where Borneo is today. It has taken that long for the earth's tectonic plates to haul Britain from the equator to these temperate northern latitudes. Warm sub-tropical seas teemed with marine life over long periods of time. Their remains were crushed into successive sedimentary layers of limestones interspersed with the sandstones that resulted from the alluvial sand deposits of vast slow moving rivers. Limestone is less resistant than the intervening layers of sandstone. Geological sections carefully studied from the later lead mines in Weardale show many successive layers of each, and hybrid bands of mudstones and shales. Weardale drew this attention because of the later value of lead ores found in later mineral-rich intrusions into the sedimentary rock beds.

Sandstone is the predominant surface rock through the Shire, defining the 700-900ft plateau sloping gently eastwards, but lower layers are revealed where the sandstone has been dissected by water. The less-resistant limestone has washed away much more easily than sandstone through the action of water over millions of years, leaving us those deep gorges of high sandstone crags above shale and limestone. Water action has washed lots of fossils downstream, relics of those tropical seas of 300 million years ago, and now occasionally found in local streams such as the Rowley Burn.

The Carboniferous sequence is traditionally concluded with the dense swamps of tropical forest, the origins of the great coalfields. Sedimentary beds were tilted to the east over millions of years. Most of the higher strata have been eroded away, most notably the coal deposits, which predominantly remain now only much nearer the coast – in West Durham, on Tyneside and northwards – before dipping under the North Sea. There is, however, a local exception to this as a result of a significant fault-line running east to west roughly along the line of the Tyne valley – the Stublick

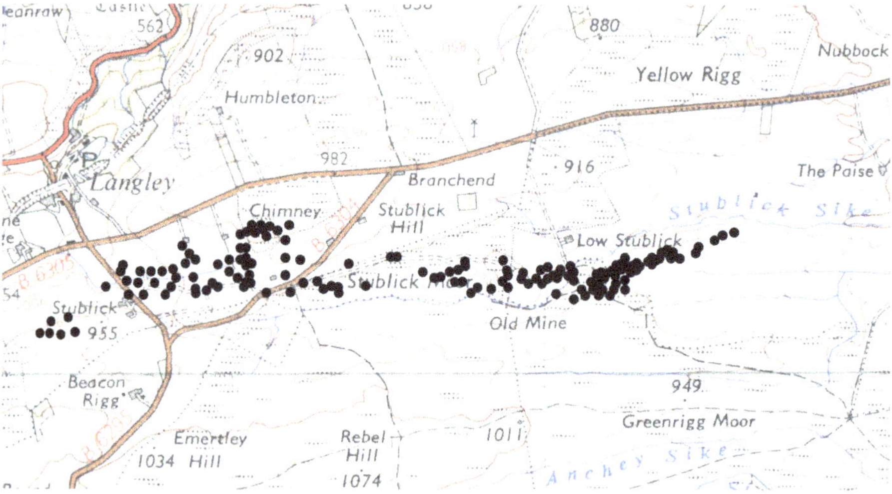

Figs 7 (top) and 8: The pockmarked remains of coal pits mark out the line of the Stublick fault west of Hexham

Fault. To the north the rock was thrown downwards, which meant coal beds still remain at or close to the surface. These have been worked in recent centuries. The scars left by small-scale coalpits can still be seen at Stublick, at the western end of the Dipton Burn's catchment (see Figures 7 and 8). There was a significant mine just north of the Tyne at Acomb until a century or so ago. One of the Tyne crossings just west of Hexham was named Coleford in the 16th century.[1] The prevailing eastward tilt of the sedimentary rockbeds explains why many streams flow in that direction and only a few run short and fast to the west. Within the Devil's Water catchment there is far more land to the west of the river than to the east.

In the last million years or so, the action of repeated periods of glaciation have left their mark as ice sheets advanced and then retreated across northern England. Glaciers scoured away a huge amount of bedrock, and left us with the smooth profile of the hills today. The most recent retreat of the ice was some 11,000 years ago. As the ice smoothed out and lowered the higher peaks it dumped the scoured-out material on lower ground. Striking visible signs remain today in the form of drumlins of glacial deposit from Rawgreen to Whitley Chapel. Low hills of quite sandy material are revealed by rabbit burrows or soil slumps where the grass has worn away. Aydon Shields farm is built on one, and just to its north lies the most prominent, Black Hill, opposite Mire House. The stream that runs down between them is the Cobble Burn, revealingly named after the smooth rounded stones carried down by the ice. St. Helen's church appears to sit on another of these hillocks, and the bicycle track on the sports field exploits the next. Up to six yards of drift deposit or till was carried and dumped by glaciers onto the lower ground.

When each ice sheet started to recede an enormous volume of glacial meltwater was released, often cutting deep new channels through existing valley sides. Rowantree Cleugh, near the southern edge of the Shire, is a very distinctive valley which today looks far too big for the trickle of the burn that runs eastwards towards Harwood Shield. Like the nearby Beldon Cleugh (see Figure 9) it has the appearance of a double ended valley. The likeliest explanation is that they were created by glacial meltwater. Pressure of ice or meltwater in a huge lake in the upper Derwent Valley created a northwards outlet at the upper end of an originally south-facing valley. This allowed a cascade of water to descend that greatly deepened the Devil's Water valley. It cut a gorge through the shale below Long Lee, running through Steelcrags Wood, and probably accounts for the deep channel along much of the length of the valley.[2] Much of the northward drainage into the Tyne valley from the Northern Pennines runs through noticeably deep ravines, such as in the Devil's Water catchment, the Allen valley below Cupola Bridge, and the burns running down through Hexham. Most of the Shire's streams are still cutting down through sandstone to the less resistant shale and limestone beds. Fast flowing burns fall over the sandstone ledges creating occasional waterfalls – the 'land of singing waters', such as along the gorge of the Dipton Burn west of the Dipton Mill.

Meltwater from each ebbing ice age deposited sands and gravel in the river valleys, finer material than the glacial till. These alluvial deposits stand as high terraces above the present river levels. Hexham is built on one. In the Shire two distinct terraces can be seen across the road from Low Staples, probably representing successive deposits of alluvium, which were cut by later river action to leave steeper banks between them. On stretches of the Devil's Water and its main tributaries wide areas of

Fig 9 (top): The double ended glacial valley of Beldon Cleugh looking north
Fig 10 (above): River terraces cut by the Devil's Water below Red Lead Mill, probably as a result of the river deepening following the release of glacial meltwater

alluvial soil dumping have given us haughs, sheltered land with rich soil but dangerously prone to flooding as rivers changed their course along the valley floors. Work by geographers and soil scientists on the River Tyne have shown that only in the last 200-300 years have the main river courses become more securely entrenched.[3] This 1774 description is probably typical of earlier times:

> *'The Devil's Water which is very rapid and sudden in its spates, frequently takes away a great part of the waste land of this farm [old Peacock House, just east of Litharge] adjoining to it, and there is a small piece which has been separated from Whitefield by the above river's having made itself a new channel now claimed by Job Ward who owns the land on the opposite side. It is not possible, without going to very considerable expense, to secure the Land against the attacks of this rageing river'.*[4]

In the early 20th century the river eroded enough of the steep bank north of Ordley to undermine the lane that ran down through the small settlement and on towards Newbiggin. The lane was replaced by the wide and straight 'Ordley bypass' of today. Just to the north of Dalton the course of the Ham Burn is already different to that shown on the first edition OS map surveyed in 1860, and empty dry channels can be seen on the banks of the current course of the stream.

The underlying geology of the Shire gives rise to poor acidic soil, heavy clay that does not drain well and is hard to work. The most important legacy of glacial action is that the material eroded, churned and dumped at lower levels is generally better drained brown earth and is easier to work. But none of it is as fertile as that in the Tyne Valley or the eastern Northumberland plains.

This all helped to form the fundamental character of the landscape. Altitude and latitude also have a bearing on how the land has been exploited. England generally has seven to eight months above the six degrees centigrade needed for plant growth, but in northern uplands this falls to five or six months. Until quite recently this will have been short enough to make life precarious and marginal, as if poor soils weren't difficult enough. And it also means that slight variations in average temperatures had a much more marked effect on the local environment than in lowland Britain.

To start with, as the ice retreated 11,000 years ago, temperatures increased fairly quickly, and to a level around three to four degrees centigrade higher than today.[5] Pollen analysis from elsewhere in the region shows that permafrost and tundra were succeeded by grasses and then woodland, predominantly oak and hazel in the north. Some of this ancient woodland is reflected in later placenames – Hesleywell/ hazel, embley/elmley – an elm clearing. Alder will have grown in the boggy valleys. Birch fragments found on Allendale Common show that even the now bare moorland tops carried woods, although there is some debate among historians of ecology as to whether this will have been dense, unbroken forest or woodland patches with open glades. This will have mattered to the pattern of grazing of the big game, moving northwards as the climate improved – and the first human hunting groups that followed them.

[1] W Nicholson. (ed) *Leges Marchiarum or Border Laws,* (1705), pp.172-3.
[2] J B Sissons, 'Sub-glacial stream erosion in Southern Northumberland', *Scottish Geographical Journal,* 74-3, (1958).
[3] D Passmore and M Macklin, 'Geoarchaeology of the Tyne Basin: Holocene River Valley Environments and the Archaeological Record', in C Tolan-Smith (ed), *Landscape Archaeology in Tynedale,* (1997).
[4] Greenwich Hospital Visitation report, 1774: TNA ADM 79/57 p.70.
[5] I Simmons & M Tooley, *The Environment in British Prehistory,* (1981).

2. Prehistory

The archaeological record across the country as a whole shows that as the climate warmed up, following the retreat of the ice, people were never far behind. It is often hard for us to relate to such distant ancestors, particularly when the only traces left are a few basic hand tools, but these were people pretty much anatomically identical to ourselves, with the same brain capacity. They lacked the dozens of generations' worth of inherited knowledge available to us now but I think we would recognise their tenacity, inventiveness and adventure in the face of hostile conditions. In the absence of our intricate far-flung web of inter-dependence, their ability to live on their wits was probably noticeably superior to our own.

We generally mark the progress of prehistoric humanity by the increasing sophistication of the stone tools and hunting weapons found. The 'stone age' is traditionally divided between the old (Paleolithic – up to 12,000 years ago in Britain), middle (Mesolithic, 12-6,000 years ago, ie. after the most recent ice age) and new (Neolithic, 6,000 to 4,000 years ago) eras accordingly. For the Shire, the evidence of human activity from this period is very thin, but it's worth considering an interesting small area right on the southern boundary, between the Devil's Water and the Derwent: the high ground of Birkside Fell and the wide ridge at Blackburn Head, at about 1,200ft (365m) altitude. From here there are wide views to the distant blue horizons, dominated in the north by the distinctive profiles of the Simonside Hills and the Cheviot, 30 and 45 miles away respectively.

It's here that the first trace of human presence in the area has been found so far. Hundreds of late Mesolithic worked flint cores and tools were discovered eroding from the exposed peat. Judging from their style they possibly date from between 5000 and 4000BC. From at least this period, and probably much earlier, people are known to have sought out good sources of flint, chert and quartz for toolmaking and to have traded them over long distances.[1] A keen eyed hunter must have found this site on an expedition to the fells some 6-7,000 years ago, perhaps following herds to the ridge top or over the col between the valleys on their seasonal migrations.

Just a mile northeast a 'longman's grave' is shown on the OS map, not far from that Mesolithic tool site on Birkside, the name suggesting a Neolithic burial in a long barrow. A leaf-shaped arrow-head from this period was found about a mile further north.[2] Neolithic people were the first farmers in Britain. From around 6,000 years ago, instead of relying on hunting for meat and gathering wild produce, livestock were domesticated and many crops cultivated. This could support permanent settlement, and

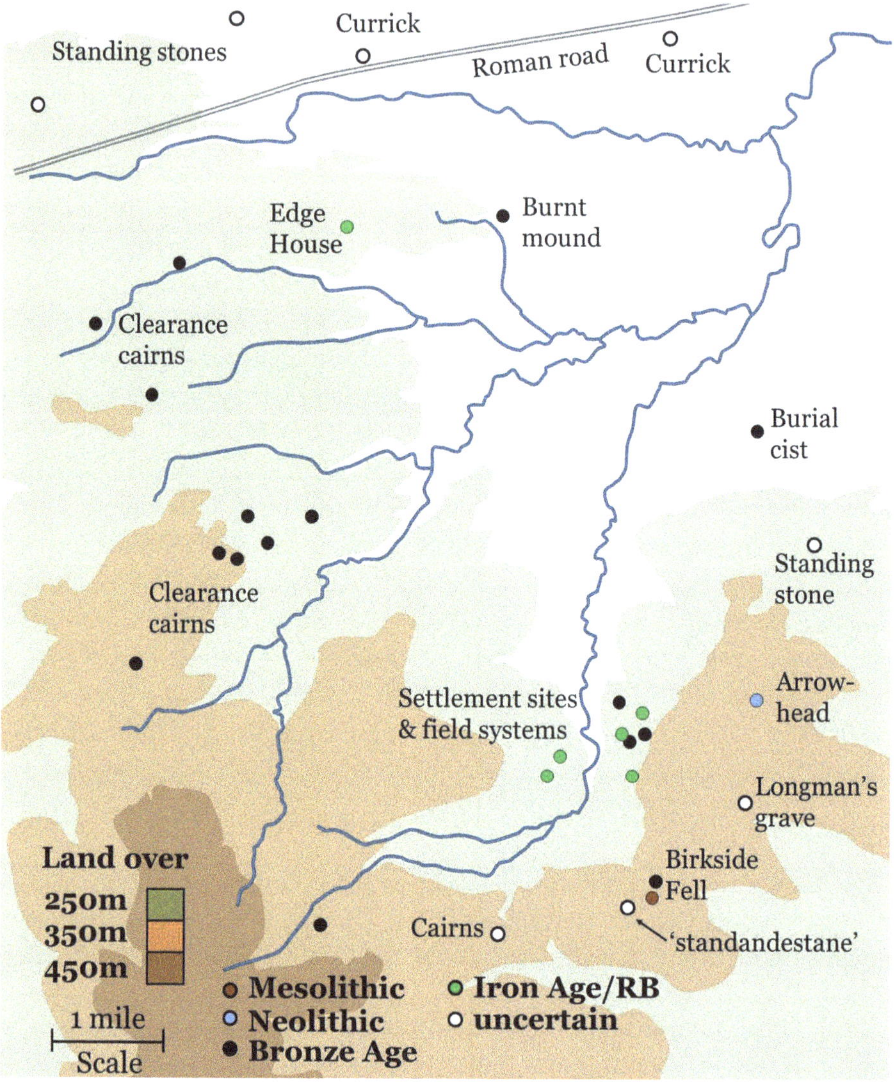

Fig 11: Prehistoric sites in Hexhamshire

a large increase in population. It would be entirely natural for the effort committed to clearing trees for cultivation and pasture using smooth stone Neolithic axes to be accompanied by a desire to own and demarcate land for the first time. Interestingly a Blanchland charter from 1214, describing a boundary running along that same ridge between the Devil's Water catchment and the Derwent, included the 'Standandestane' – a standing stone – as one of the landmarks.[3] These too can date from Neolithic times, one of the ways for people intentionally to leave a visible permanent mark on the landscape, signifying both religious belief and a need to mark out territory.

However, a single 'longman's grave' placename – without any sign of the grave itself – and the medieval mention of a long-lost standing stone -which might well have dated from later times do not demonstrate Neolithic activity on Birkside Fell. There is little evidence of Neolithic occupation in the wider area around the Shire or outside the far north of Northumberland. The slight trace of a possible circular henge feature, usually associated with the Neolithic period, was identified near Allendale a few years ago, but this has yet to be fully investigated.[4] From what we have learned from archaeology in the area to date it seems Britain's first farmers concentrated their activity elsewhere.

We can be much more confident that the high ground around the south of the Shire was settled and farmed by skilled metal-using people with the knowledge of fusing copper with tin to make bronze tools and weapons. The most complete prehistoric find on the high land of Birkside Fell to date is of a Bronze Age burial. It lay in the centre of the remains of a wide cairn, ringed by a kerb of stones, right on the col on Birkside Fell near Blackburn Head (see Figure 12). Cremated remains of two adults in the complete and carefully buried fine pottery urn were found and excavated by archaeologist Chris Tolan-Smith in the 1990s. They have been dated to around 1700-2000BC.[5] It seems likely from recent genetic evidence that metal working – initially of copper – was brought to Britain by people from continental Europe from around 2500BC.[6] There are many remains of their roundhouses and small square fields in north and central Northumberland, and rock art that probably dates from a similar time or earlier. This fits with the pattern of evidence seen elsewhere across Britain of increasingly advanced metalwork, tools, farming and higher population densities during the Bronze Age.

Prehistoric remains were surveyed in the 1990s on the land below Birkside Fell northwards towards Burntshield Haugh, and today part of the Lord Crewe estate. Some of the features identified probably belong to a later period, but possibly overlaid earlier work in the Bronze Age to clear stones into cairns to improve the grazing and enable the land to be worked for crops. This is all on the fellside visible eastwards from Lillswood. Walking on the ground today shows how many sites were located carefully on shallow west- and south-facing terraces near springs, about 900ft (275m) above sea level. One or two possible burial cists – effectively stone boxes, characteristic of the Bronze Age – lie half buried near a more recent sheepfold. Did these remains belong to the same community that created the ring cairn at Blackburn Head, and another further west, near Beldon Cleugh?

Perhaps that lost standing stone on the ridge was erected by the

Fig 12: Ring cairn on Birkside Fell

same Bronze Age inhabitants. Other possible standing stones have been recorded, in recent times, near Ladycross Quarry, at 1,120ft altitude and lower down the same north-facing slope in Black Plantation, but they are impossible to date with any certainty. However, that 13th century record of a standing stone on the watershed ridge shows that it, at least, was a well-recognised landmark then. There is a good chance it had already stood there for three thousand years, a prominent landmark silhouetted on the horizon in low winter sun and by thousands of full moons crossing the southern sky, until some medieval farmer was brave enough to defy ancestral ghosts and take it down to use as a gatepost or house footing. But for full dramatic effect it had to be visible. The ridge and its flanks must have been clear of trees, and might have been since those Mesolithic hunters knapped flints there. Excavations of Mesolithic sites in which waterlogged timber was preserved show that woodland was actively managed. Ancient wildwood was probably burned or felled to allow new straight trunk growth useful for timber, or to create groves of new shoots attractive to their prey and to provide good sightlines for spears and arrows.

This process was accelerated with the arrival of farming, trees being felled by Neolithic stone axes and by their much more effective bronze successors. Possible Bronze Age sites have been documented elsewhere on the high ground to the west, between Hexhamshire and Allendale. A cairnfield of stones cleared on Greenrigg moor implies that the land was to be tilled to grow crops. A burial cairn and a clearance cairn two miles south on Burntridge Moor are probably also of similar vintage. These sites are at 950ft (290m) and 1,120ft (340m) altitude respectively.[7] As with Birkside Fell the clear implication is that the growing season was long enough to support pastoral or even arable farming at such heights in northern fell country three to four thousand years ago. From what we can tell of the climate record, temperatures fell slowly from the heights reached at around 4000BC (3-4°C above present levels) but were evidently still high enough to support farming that would hardly be viable there today.

The identification of such landscape features used to rely entirely on observation on the ground. From the mid-20th century this was supplemented by aerial photography. This allowed wider areas to be surveyed but was still selective in coverage. High definition satellite imagery such as that used by Google Earth is much more comprehensive but still relies on light and ground conditions to assist identification. A recent breakthrough has come with the availability of LiDaR (light detection and ranging) imagery. This involves aerial sensors bouncing laser beams onto the land surface below in order to build up a 3D representation. The resulting images can then be manipulated to pick out ground features too subtle to be identified by aerial photography. One such survey, using Environment Agency LiDaR imagery available for the Allen Valleys and Hexhamshire, was carried out as part of the North Pennines AONB Altogether Archaeology project in the 2010s. It has provided many new insights into the development of the Shire's landscape that are drawn upon elsewhere in this book, but revealed very little that could have survived from the Bronze Age. However, two possible burnt mounds have been identified next to a minor stream at 820ft (250m) altitude on Dotland Fell.[8] Excavations of burnt mounds elsewhere have shown they typically consist of a hearth and trough possibly used to heat stones and water for unclear purposes. They mostly date from the middle (1900-1500BC) and late (1200-800BC) Bronze Age.

The absence of other surviving features from this period in the local landscape does not mean that Bronze Age human activity was restricted to the higher land. A stone-sided burial chamber or cist, typical of the early to middle Bronze Age (c.2000BC) was disturbed by a plough on a low ridge at 600ft altitude (185m) near Dukesfield Hall in 2011.[9] This was a chance find on ploughed land, and the later intensive development of lowland areas could well have wiped out virtually all traces of earlier prehistoric activity. As with 'longman's grave' it is possible that some features survived long enough to live on in placenames or the documentary record. A 'currack of stones' – a cairn – mentioned in a 1755 survey of the land to be enclosed on Hexham Common – was evidently distinctive enough towards the east end of the ridge north of the Dipton Burn at Beacon Hill to be used as a landmark when setting out the road west of Ochrelands today.[10] However impressive in its time, it is impossible to date, but the land here had been open common land since at least medieval times and does not mark any boundary line known in recorded history. Interestingly, Watch Currick farm (created and so-named after the 1755 enclosure) and 'Currick Hill' stand at the western end of the same ridge. Other curricks were noted further west on a 1735 map of the south-east to north-west boundary between Nubbock and Elrington, to the north of which the land drops quite steeply towards the Tyne Valley. The possibility remains that these lost cairns (at between 690 and 890ft in altitude) marked boundaries or early field clearance, or both, dating from the Bronze Age.

These are isolated observations, mostly resting upon the most slender of suppositions. However, there is another source of evidence suggesting that Bronze Age farming elsewhere in the region remained predominantly in the hills – the analysis of pollen cores. Vertical soil samples taken from damp ground can preserve an organic record of the pollen dispersed by vegetation through time, and the approximate dates at which significant changes took place can often be established. They can therefore indicate roughly when primeval woodland was replaced by grassland and cereals, marking the advance of agriculture – and sometimes also its retreat. One such pollen core taken from Pow Hill in the nearby Derwent valley suggests that woodland remained in the valley until well after the Bronze Age.[11] It then appears to have been cleared in the last few centuries BC, when a much more effective metal was available to hack at the trees: iron. Until then, perhaps, the general Bronze Age land-use pattern in areas such as the Shire was for settlement, cultivation and stock pasturing to be concentrated mainly on the higher plateaus, leaving dense woodland in the valleys.

The chances are that the Bronze Age was followed by several centuries of abandonment. Climatic conditions seem to have deteriorated from about 1200BC with colder and wetter weather. One theory has it that this cooling was linked to the eruption of Mt Hekla in Iceland in 1159 BC, which dispersed clouds of volcanic material southwards over Britain. In any case, colder and wetter conditions would have had a marked effect on marginal uphill land such as in the Shire. Much further south, on Dartmoor, it appears that extensive and long-established field systems incorporating boundaries known as reaves deteriorated or were even abandoned towards the end of the second millennium BC. If so, it is unlikely that conditions were any more conducive to agriculture in the northern uplands. Cold and wet conditions continued, possibly interrupted by some brief improvements, until around 200-100BC. The renewed signs in the pollen and archaeological record of human activity potentially date from around this time. Even if this occurred a century or two earlier, as suggested by pollen data and excavation in Swaledale, it is still possible that few people lived in or made much use of the Shire's resources for the best part of a thousand years.

This would easily have been long enough for woodland to have recolonised any previously cleared land on the better soils at lower altitudes. But on the poorly drained fell tops, wetter climatic conditions had probably long discouraged the survival of tree cover.[12] Human intervention, whether by Bronze Age settlers or their Mesolithic and Neolithic predecessors, might only have assisted rather than initiated this process. Never very deep or fertile on the sandstone felltops, the soil was probably ill-suited to cultivation and provided only poor grazing. There was no woodland regeneration. Peat deposits began to form on the poorly drained acidic land. Heather growth will have followed. This process was certainly underway on Birkside Fell before the burial urn was set into the peat between 2000BC and 1700BC, and possibly from soon after the flint remains were dropped by the Mesolithic hunters before 4000BC.[13] But if peat was forming by the time of that burial any cultivation on the fell had already been abandoned. Today's great sweep of heather-clad moorland, purple under the August sun, could well be the result of natural climate change several thousand years ago, helped along by prehistoric forest clearance. How many traces of those early visitors and inhabitants are sealed under the deep peat formation around the high southern rim of the Shire?

As the climate pendulum swung back again, it heralded a warmer period of several hundred years' duration, encompassing the later Iron Age and the Roman Empire in Britain. Iron rarely appeared in Britain before around 600BC. If well-made it was stronger and lighter than bronze, but prone to rust. One of its principal advantages was that iron was much more widely available as a raw material compared to the tin and copper needed for bronze. This effectively made it cheap enough to obtain, smelt and forge for widespread use. It was therefore available to a higher proportion of the population to fell trees, dress timber, till ground – and to fight with. Perhaps this, in conjunction with environmental conditions that, while improving, were not as benign as in the high Bronze Age, helps to explain why Iron Age roundhouses were typically found in twos and threes within roughly squared (rectilinear) defensible enclosures. Many of the more prominent hilltops were fortified with dramatic banks and ditches during this period, such as at Warden Hill, overlooking the confluence of the North and South Tyne.

The Iron Age is normally said to have ended in Britain with the Roman invasion in 43AD. The Romans have left our first written records, traditionally marking the line between prehistory and history. Within the area of Roman occupation the native population is usually called Romano-British from this point onwards, but these labels apply to the same people, tribes who would surely have identified in the same way either side of the arrival of the legions. Following the conquest, achieved through violence in some places and peaceful agreement in others, there would certainly have been changes, and opportunities for the supply of food and trade. Those defensive ditches around Warden Hill appear to have been reduced, and are overlain by house platforms. But it is hardly surprising that the form of that housing seems largely unchanged from before. Except where excavations discover small artefacts of clear Roman provenance, perhaps the remains of local trading, there is little to distinguish between 'Iron Age' and 'Romano-British' native settlements either side of the conquest. Henceforth, therefore, they are merged here into the clumsy but handy label of 'Iron Age/RB'. I use it to cover the late first millennium BC to the end of the Roman occupation in the early 5th century AD.

As with Mesolithic and Bronze Age features, there are remains of later prehistoric occupation below Birkside Fell on the slopes east of Burntshield Haugh. Four probable settlement sites typical of the Iron Age/RB period – one or two small circular house platforms inside a rectilinear enclosure – have been identified through ground and LiDaR survey, along with adjacent contemporary field boundaries. If they are the remains of people moving back into the area after centuries of cold abandonment then those returning settlers would probably have found that further peat formation on the highest ground had left it fit for little more than very rough grazing. Cultivation would have required woodland clearance at lower altitudes, as appears to have been the case in the nearby Derwent valley and elsewhere – presumably with the aid of iron tools.[14] A study of the Prudhoe area has identified what appear to be the remains of Iron Age/RB field systems and other features in the lowland Tyne valley.[15] This would mean that much Iron Age/RB activity on the lower ground is invisible to

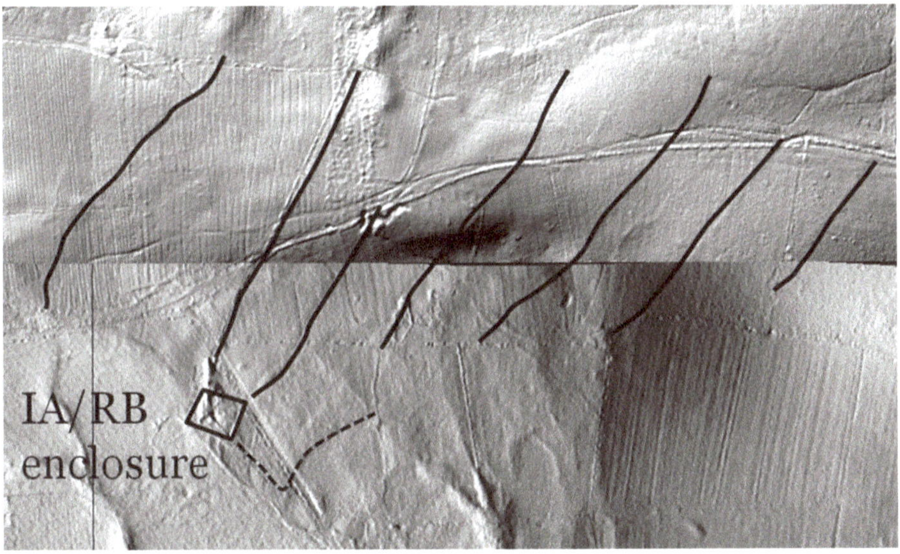

Fig 13 (top): LiDaR image of the Edge House Iron Age/RB settlement and field system, with overlain interpretation to emphasise the key features
Fig 14 (above): The Edge House settlement enclosure, from west

us today, erased by extensive reworking of the land during the last two thousand years. Nevertheless, some further traces have survived. The Shire LiDaR survey identified two probable Iron Age/RB settlements just to the west of Burntshield Haugh across the Devil's Water, near Hesleywell and New House.[16]

Another site from this period lies north-westwards across the Shire near Edge House. It probably owes its survival to being located on high ground – at 900ft altitude (275m) – that was open common land until 1800, and not intensively farmed in recent centuries. This rectangular enclosure – an earth bank and ditch – containing at least three round huts was identified as an Iron Age/RB site by the archaeologist George Jobey in the 1970s.[17] It is clearly visible on Google Earth, and now that LiDaR imagery is also available (see Figure 13) a series of at least seven roughly parallel boundaries of a co-axial field system can be seen running north-eastwards, 40-60 metres apart. Two of them clearly respect the settlement enclosure, and they all lie under later boundaries and tracks. Faint signs of Iron Age/RB ploughing – known as cord rig – have been observed, aligned with the co-axial banks.[18] Although used only for rough grazing today, the land into which the banks run was described as 'breckony beds' in the 1759 Dotland Common enclosure award and bracken tends to grow on decent soil.[19] Perhaps this explains why the land at such a height was worth cultivating in a climate that would have been distinctly cooler than during the Bronze Age. Furthermore, raising rigs can aerate and warm the soil. Nevertheless, better land was surely also available to be cleared by Iron Age/RB farmers at lower altitudes, so for Edge House to be cultivated suggests there was high demand for food grains.

This perhaps implied a high local population by the end of the prehistoric era. Even if not, we can be reasonably confident that the close proximity of a major Roman military supply base for the Hadrian's Wall garrison at Corbridge generated strong demand for agricultural produce from at least the 2nd century AD. A mile to the north of Edge House, a 2016 project drew further attention to this possibility. Having identified what appeared to be the straight lines of a Roman road across the high land south-west of Hexham using LiDaR images, the Altogether Archaeology group excavated sections of it near Stublick and Watch Currick farms that summer. Although nothing was found to date it securely, the profile of surviving stonework and ditching is entirely consistent with Roman construction. It appears to head south-westwards in the direction of Whitley Castle, a Roman fort in the South Tyne valley near Alston. The alignment of the road as it crosses the present-day racecourse road takes it precisely to the southern end of the Roman bridge across the Tyne at Corbridge, which had connections to the trunk network of major roads north and south.[20] It is a potentially important addition to the map of Roman Tynedale, and means there was a decent quality supply road from the northern edge of the Shire direct to the strategic military base of the northern frontier garrison, just four miles away.

This surely meant that ground suitable for farming for miles around

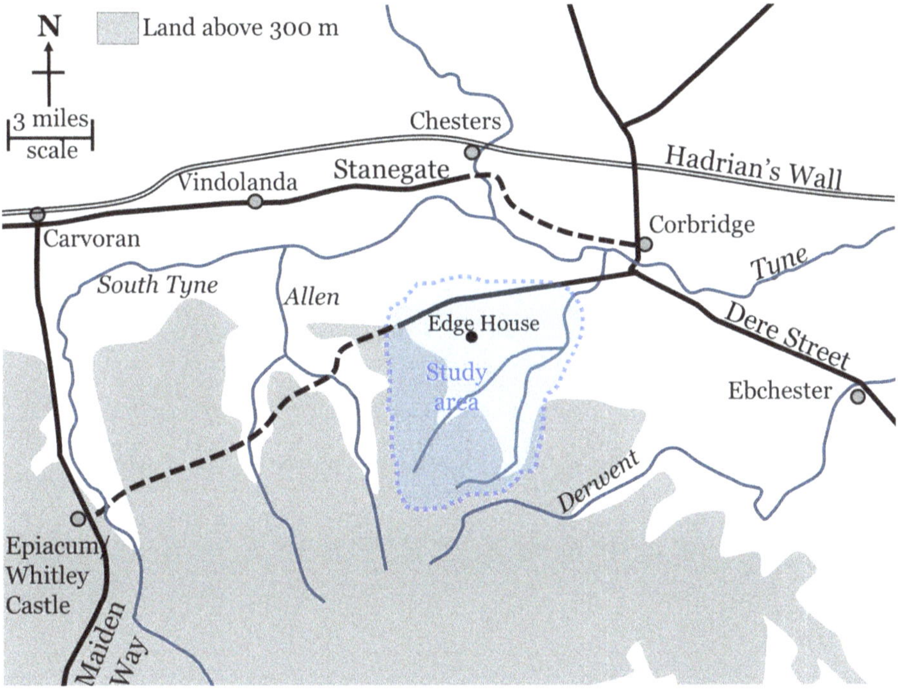

Fig 15: Roman roads, including the recently identified road from Corbridge to Epiacum, sections of which were excavated in the Stublick area in 2016

must have been used to produce grain and livestock, even if all trace of it has since been lost because of later re-use of both the land and of any building stone. Seen in this context, and despite the mediocre fertility of its soil, the south facing land of Black Hill, Plover Hill, Peterel Field, Queen's Letch and Oakerland, right next to a road with direct and close access to the Roman town and military supply base, was surely intensively farmed during the heyday of Roman occupation. Yet apart from the hesitant identification on the Northumberland HER of a sub-rectangular enclosure in cropmarks on an aerial photo on the haugh just north of Newbiggin bridge, there are no clues on the ground today.[21] Any surface traces would have been swept away when this previously open common ground was enclosed in the 1750s into the geometric pattern we see today, and the land improved. Perhaps ground penetrating radar survey and trial excavations near the spring line on this hillside will one day reveal more.

There are scarcely any direct traces of Roman presence in the Shire. Some bronze and silver coins of Roman vintage are said to have been discovered in the 1980s at Dotland. Commanding open views to north, east and south (assuming the land was clear of tree cover) this possibly provided a suitable lookout post, if one was thought necessary, perhaps in similar fashion to the one identified at Staward Pele next to the Allen gorge.[22] The discovery in 2009 by a metal-detectorist of a Trajan silver denarius dated 116-117AD near the co-axial field system beyond Edge House is arguably of greater interest. Perhaps lost on the way home from selling produce at Corbridge, its recent discovery could help to tie the marking out, clearing and working of that high farmland to the vast demands of the Roman military machine.[23]

[1] C Tolan-Smith, 'A Cairn on Birkside Fell – Excavations in 1996 and 1997', *AA*, 5th ser., 34, (2005), p.16.

[2] HER site reference N8401.

[3] HN-6, pp.313-4.

[4] AVH, p.26

[5] It can be seen in the Great North Museum in Newcastle. C Tolan-Smith, *op cit.*

[6] T Booth *et al*, 'Tales from the Supplementary Information: Ancestry Change in Chalcolithic–Early Bronze Age Britain Was Gradual with Varied Kinship Organization', *Cambridge Archaeological Journal*, 31-3, (2021).

[7] HER sites N27836, N7455.

[8] AVH, p.36.

[9] HER site N24840.

[10] Hexham Common enclosure award, May 1755: NRO QRD/2. The highest point along this section of the road is by a small covered water reservoir at NY936624.

[11] J Turner & J Hodgson, 'Studies in the Vegetational History of the Northern Pennines:II. An Atypical Pollen Diagram from Pow Hill, Co. Durham', *Journal of Ecology*, Vol 69-1, (1981), pp. 177, 182, 185. A similar pattern was observed at Fotherley Moss two miles east of Slaley at 650ft altitude (200m).

[12] A Gallego-Sala et al, 'Climate-driven expansion of blanket bogs in Britain during the Holocene', *Climate of the Past Discussions*, 11-5, (2015).

[13] C Ivory, 'A geoarchaeological approach to understanding archaeological context in an upland landscape' Newcastle University MA dissertation, 1997

[14] Derwent valley: pollen core from Pow Hill: Turner & Hodgson, *op cit*; Horsley wood in eastern Tynedale was possibly cleared at a similar time: M Tolan-Smith, 'The Medieval Landscape 1: Approaches to the Study of Ancient Woodland – Horsley Wood', in *Landscape Archaeology in Tynedale, op cit.* Further south, woodland in Swaledale was cleared in the middle Iron Age: A Fleming, *Swaledale, Valley of the Wild River*, (2010), pp.145-7.

[15] S Cousins, 'The Prudhoe Landscape History Project: A Retrogressive Study of the Landscape History of Part of Southern Northumberland', in T Faulkner, H Berry & J Gregory (eds), *Northern Landscapes. Representations and Realities of North-East England*, (2010) pp.37-8.

[16] AVH, pp.32-3.

[17] G Jobey, *A Field Guide to Prehistoric Northumberland: Pt. 2*, (1974), p.32.

[18] M Green, *pers comm.*

[19] Dotland Common Enclosure award. NRO 11619.

[20] M Green & G Finch, 'A Roman road southwest from Corbridge?', *HH*, 27, (2017)

[21] HER site N8784.

[22] E Birley, 'A Roman Altar from Staward Pele, and Roman Remains in Allendale', *AA*, 4th ser, 28, (1950), p.141.

[23] Portable Antiquities Scheme finds database: https://finds.org.uk/database/artefacts/record/id/284946.

3. Tides of medieval change

Ebb – the Dark Ages

The long period characterised as medieval was, very roughly, the millennium between the departure of the Roman legions and the advent of the Tudors in the late 15th century. It might, equally simplistically, be seen as a long flowing tide of advance across the landscape between two much shorter ebbing tides of retreat. The first of these 'ebb tides' followed in the wake of the withdrawal of Roman legions to the continent in the 410s, leaving local auxiliary units to figure out their own future.

No longer could there have been such strong local demand for food and other army supplies. The ensuing two centuries or so are still often referred to as the 'Dark Ages', with a presumption of the collapse of society until the arrival of Anglo-Saxon invaders from the 6th century. Recent scholarship is sceptical of such stark claims.[1] The absence of written records does not necessarily mean a rapid collapse into anarchy. Britain was quite possibly more heavily populated when Roman control ended than at the time of the Norman conquest and Domesday Book 650 years later. But without documentary evidence and given the difficulty of dating scarce archaeological remains from these centuries, we have little to go on with regard to the course of settlement and land use in our region. What we can say is that the climate deteriorated again in the 6th century. Alongside much colder and wetter weather there are suspicions that plague devastated the population of Britain and continental Europe in the mid-6th century.[2]

If there was a dark age in Northumberland this was it – perhaps 150 years of decline, social breakdown and a retreat from the inhospitable hills. The Iron Age/RB remains at Edge House and above Burntshield Haugh are probably still visible because the land was abandoned at some stage after the end of Roman rule and never worked as intensively again. The broad south-facing slope below the racecourse ridge could have been cultivated for the Corbridge military base, but there is no record of any further use of the majority of it until it was enclosed as part of Hexham Common in the 1750s. Then there is the fate of the presumed Roman road that traversed the ridge on its way to Corbridge. Although not visible on LiDaR east of Watch Currick, its route must have taken it through the racecourse grounds at Yarridge, an island of cultivation reclaimed from the common in the early 12th century (of which more later). An estate map of 1802 which appears to preserve some medieval features shows no recognition whatsoever of the likely course of the presumed Roman road. This presumably meant that its course was lost by the time Yarridge was taken in from the wasteland along the ridge in the 1110s or even earlier.[3] The apparent disappearance of a good quality level road suggests that the high and windswept ground it crosses south of Hexham was completely abandoned in the years after the departure of the Roman legions. We don't know if the Shire was completely depopulated, for the land might have been used by the descendants of the Romano-British inhabitants for low-intensity grazing under thinly-spread trees – wood pasture. However, there would have been far better land for smaller communities to work down in the Tyne Valley, where the growing season was also longer.

If any farmland was given up for even just a century it would be difficult to recognise as such after the silent return of oak, elm, hazel and alder. This, perhaps, was the general state of the valley land as farming intensified again in what is generally now referred to as the early medieval period. While we should not rush to assume that the land had been abandoned altogether, this could still be considered as a third wave of expansion of human activity and settlement in the Shire. There were possibly some English inhabitants (Angles rather than Saxons) alongside those with British ancestry, who had in turn succeeded Bronze Age farmers after an earlier gap of perhaps as much as a millennium's duration. This time they stayed. We can start identifying their impact on the landscape by peeling back later layers of development added during 15 centuries of continuous occupation and change, using the present landscape, old maps and place-names.

Flow – the long medieval expansion

Both an English presence and the re-establishment of more intensive farming is suggested by the presence of the Old English placename element '-ley'. This means a clearing, inferring the removal of tree cover. Several are still with us in the Devil's Water catchment: Houtley, Ordley, the Lee, Wooley, Whitley, Rowley (rough clearing), Ardley, Walley Thorn, Viewley, Embley (elm clearing), Hesleywell (hazel clearing), and others are known from old documents. The Steel was given as *Ruleystal* in 1233.[4] When these are plotted on a map showing the principal soil types (see Figure 16) it is interesting to note that most of them are located on the lighter and better drained soils. These are mostly near the riversides, which were eroded, churned and dumped by the glaciers. The farmers who cleared those grounds seemed able to identify the better land compared to the heavy and acidic poor clay, perhaps through observed variations in the tree cover, or simply sifting the soil by hand.

The '-ley' placenames arguably give some idea of the core of the

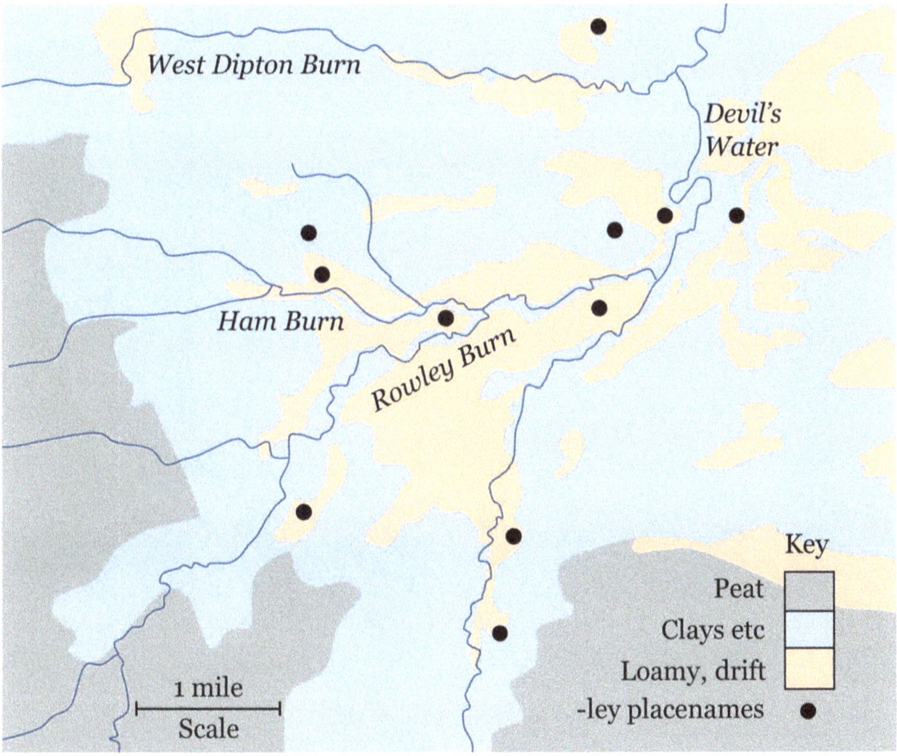

Fig 16: Soil types and '-ley' placenames

early medieval settlement and this can be married up, tentatively, with much more recent evidence. Today's map offers few obvious clues to the early pattern of settlement and farming in the post-Roman period. Much of today's field pattern dates from the enclosures of the commons since the mid-18th century, which we will turn to later. Fortunately, however, most of the plans and surveys of those enclosures have survived. While focusing on the measurement and allocation of new plots, and the course of new roads between them, they also show the boundaries of the 'antient inclosed lands'. In some cases we can go further still using early estate maps showing the pre-enclosure field systems, aerial or LiDaR imagery, and the distribution of soil types and early placenames.

Figure 17 shows the results of this speculative exercise, from which a few observations can be made. The area of enclosed and improved ground was much smaller than today's. With a few notable exceptions, which we will return to, the pre-enclosure farmsteads stayed close to the rivers. Bulbous shapes associated with individual farmsteads suggest an organic process of piecemeal clearing of woodland and rough ground for ploughing, improved grass pasture and riverside meadows. Such farmland is generally

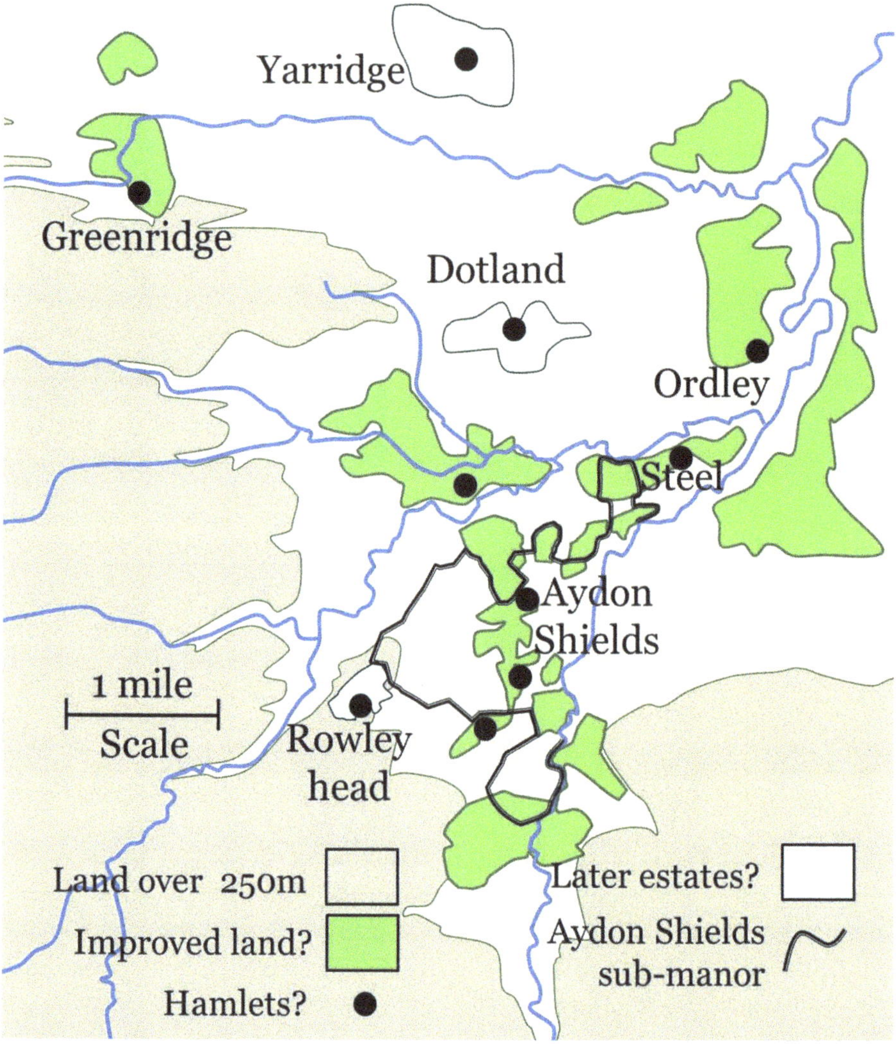

Fig 17: Speculative map of land enclosed during the early medieval re-colonisation of Hexhamshire

orientated towards Corbridge, along the line of the Devil's Water valley, even if sections of the river run through the deep Swallowship gorge. The very layout and contours of the land means Corbridge is the one town we can see from the Shire. Hexham is hidden behind the racecourse ridge. It is north of the deep ravine of the West Dipton Burn. For many centuries open fell land remained up the northern slope from this deep burn, and also down the steeper bank to Hexham itself. An ingenious map devised by the geographer Brian Roberts, based on a detailed study of placename elements, shows Corbridge at the western fringe of the Bernician 'cultural core', perhaps the heartland of settlement sustained through the post-Roman period (see Figure 18).[5] The Devil's Water valley would seem an obvious corridor of expansion and recolonization of the land.

Why then has it always been known as Hexhamshire in the historical record, rather than Corbridgeshire? Speculation on the answer is helped by considering the political and administrative background. English settlers appear to have arrived in Northumberland at some time in the 500s, establishing the kingdom of Bernicia. This came to be based at Bamburgh and expanded rapidly over the next two centuries to dominate northern England. Whether there were enough new settlers to displace the native British inhabitants is unclear. It is perhaps more likely that a small number of warriors established control over an existing population that remained in place to be taxed, and/or enslaved, and ultimately assimilated.

Evidence from several parts of Britain points towards the creation of small 'shires' in the early medieval period. Shires generally included different types of land in smaller constituent estates: from high moorland to lowland valleys, woodland, river, arable, meadow and pasture, with a central settlement to which the full range of resources available may be drawn to feed and arm the king and his warriors and supporters. Boundaries of many of them might have been long-established, inherited from British tribal units. It is worth noting in this regard that along part of the north-western boundary of Hexhamshire beyond Nubbock, and looking northwards down a steep slope into the Tyne Valley a 1770 estate map noted a standing stone, line of curricks (noted on Figure 11 above) and 'an old boundary dyke' separating the Shire from Elrington, part of the Langley Barony.[6]

Corbridge had clearly been the most important settlement in Tynedale during Roman times. The bridge could have survived into the early medieval period. It remained a royal estate until the Norman conquest. It would therefore have been an obvious focal point of a small shire (see Figure 18). If its later ecclesiastical parish boundaries are any guide, however, it was a fairly small territory of 16 square miles (42km^2) straddling the Tyne, albeit of largely fertile valley soil. Other small Bernician shires that have been identified with reasonable confidence were larger.[7] Corbridge approaches this scale (70 square miles) if combined with the two ancient parishes of Bywell to its south-east, a tract of land itself named 'Bywellshire' in the early 13th century.[8] A combined entity of Corbridge and Bywellshire has a compact and roughly triangular shape incorporating the high land of Blanchland Moor and its flanks of Birkside and Acton Fells. Immediately to the west of this putative small shire lay the later regality and parish of Hexhamshire, which included much of Allendale. The strategic importance of this land as a buffer zone protecting Corbridge from the west doubtless became clear to the Bernician King Oswald in the 630s after his defeat of the marauding British warlord Cadwalla at or near Heavenfield on Hadrian's Wall.

While the incoming Angles of the 6th century possibly found fairly empty country as soon as they moved southwards from the Tyne, there would – especially after Heavenfield – have been a strong political incentive to bring the land back into productive use. Colm O'Brien and Max Adams have observed elsewhere that early medieval rulers granted lands on the edges of cultural corelands to monasteries, with the likely expectation that the organising capability of churchmen would help bring such land into productive and taxable cultivation. The land at Hexham granted to St Wilfrid by Queen Etheldreda in 674, quite possibly within the boundaries

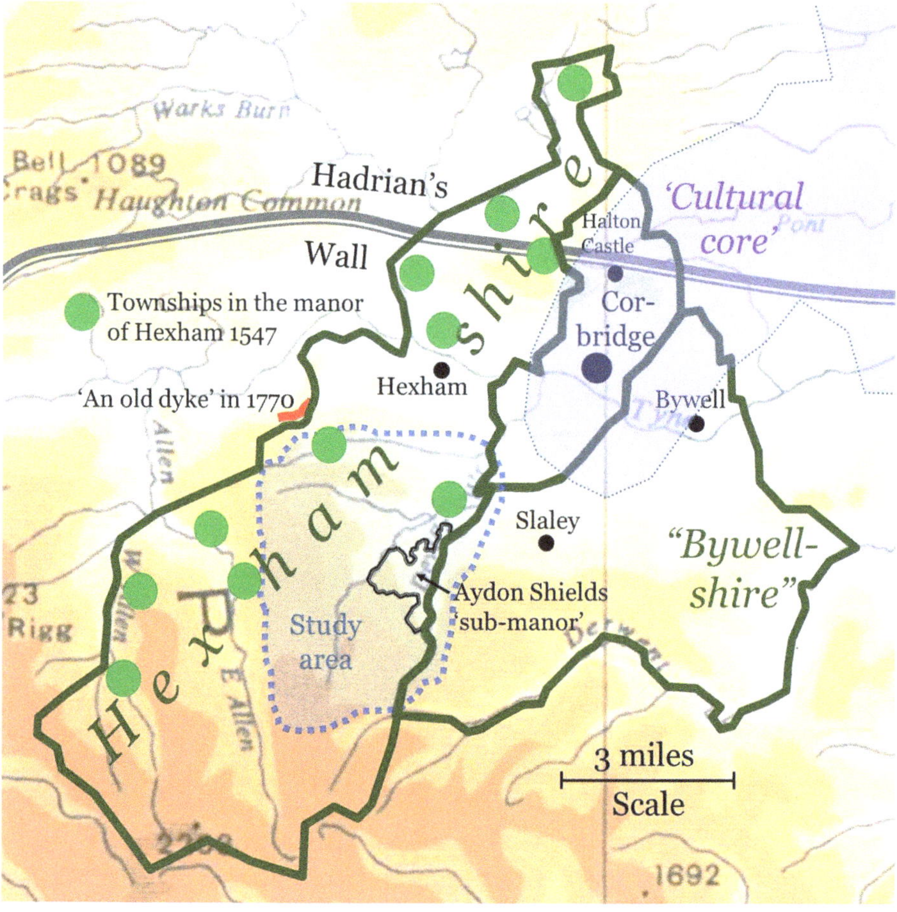

Fig 18: Early medieval Hexhamshire in regional context

Fig 19: The hamlet of Steel, *Ruleystal* in 1233

of the later regality of Hexhamshire shown in Figure 18, can perhaps be seen in this light.[9] Its 92 square miles of land to the north and south of the Tyne, of varying quality and altitude, have the character of an early medieval small shire.

The earliest written form of Hexham's name is *Hagustaldesae*, in the 8th century, possibly meaning 'the land of the warrior's son', which would be entirely logical from a strategic perspective.[10] Based on the terrace overlooking a fording point just below the Tyne confluence, a military leader could have been expected to provide a western defence against raiders, but he would need a local population to provide support to his warband and to act as a territorial reserve force if need be. But even if piecemeal settlement along the Devil's Water valley was already underway it was perhaps not enough, and the grant to St Wilfrid consequently intended to inject further energy and direct development by loyal lieutenants – 'drengs' – into a series of planned hamlet settlements on a larger scale than individual farmsteads, to be rewarded with freehold land. The 1547 survey of the Hexhamshire Regality lists sub-manors or townships that might be associated with such land grants. They largely mirror the sub-divisions used for taxation purposes in 1295. It is interesting to note that several are located towards

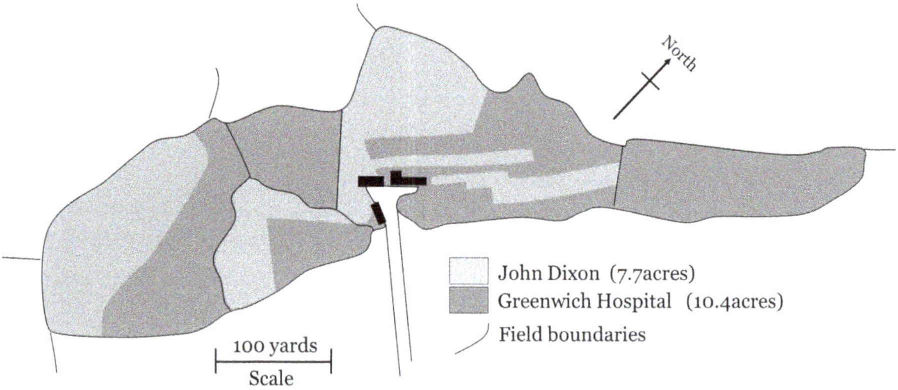

Fig 20 (top): Steel in 1802 and Fig 21: Turf House in 1800. Possible hamlets or steadings in multiple occupation with residual signs of arable strips farmed in common

the western edge of the Regality (see Figure 18), including Greenridge.[11] Effort directed at clearing and settling the land is quite likely to have used slaves captured in battles or border raids. In this respect the name Slaley – slave clearing – catches the eye, in what was once 'Bywellshire'.

Some hamlets remain. A map of the Steel in 1802 (Figure 20) is illuminating. It showed four farms with small fields and one larger area that gives the appearance of common pasture land that had been enclosed only recently. If this is removed we are left with four landholdings of 17 acres, which is roughly the size needed for a medieval household's subsistence.

Although the Shire's land was best suited to rearing cattle and sheep, it is likely that its inhabitants relied on growing most of their own crops, concentrating on spring-sown oats.[12] This remained the staple grain throughout the medieval and much of the early modern period in the Shire. Ploughing technology had a profound effect on the landscape and settlement structure. Prehistoric arable farmers barely scratched the surface of the land in their small fields with digging sticks, creating the shallow furrows of cord-rig. The gradual adoption of heavier ploughs, probably during the early medieval period, turned over a whole slice of earth, burying the weeds as it worked. But it was heavy equipment, needing a large team of oxen to drag it forward and as such normally had to be shared amongst several farmers. It also made sense to plough in long strips rather than in individual hedged fields, giving rise to larger areas of arable land sub-divided between farmers. Repeated ploughing raised riggs and deepened furrows, leaving distinctive slightly curved 'reverse S' shaped marks in the landscape. These can be seen clearly on the slope south of Dotland, but even where all trace has been removed by later agriculture, older maps and LiDaR imagery can reveal tell-tale signs of residual narrow stripfields. In 1802 at the Steel the fields no longer lay open, and many had been enlarged, but others retained an elongated pattern characteristic of open field arable land, farmed to an agreed collective rotation. Here was a block of land suitable for cultivating in common by a shared plough and ploughteam of oxen. Each household had strips within two or three open fields, leaving one fallow for a year in the hope of recovering some fertility. The 18 acres of Turf House still preserved the remnants of such arable strips in 1800 (see Figure 21).

Turf House lies just beyond the southern edge of the very interesting ancient estate of Aydon Shields. This was a substantial area of freehold land within Hexham manor occupying much of the ridge between the Rowley Burn and Devil's Water valley (see Figure 17) and for which manorial status was claimed in its own right in the 16th century. Its land lies mainly on the better soils shown in Figure 16. Aydon Shields farm sits on a prominent hill, named 'Hall hill' in 1735, from which footpaths and trackways radiate in several directions (see Figure 22). Drawing this together it is very tempting to see Aydon Shields as an early medieval Hexhamshire drengage holding.[13]

The Greenwich Hospital estate map of Aydon Shields in 1735 suggests that Aydon Shields itself and Rawgreen were early hamlets surrounded by arable strips.[14] The field names include Chapple Flatt at Aydon Shields, indicating a group of ploughed strips. Just over 60 acres of ancient land lay around Aydon Shields and 75 at Rawgreen. These would divide up neatly into four to five self-sufficient farmholdings. Rowley Head, just beyond the Aydon Shields estate, was also surrounded by 60 acres of arable land, to

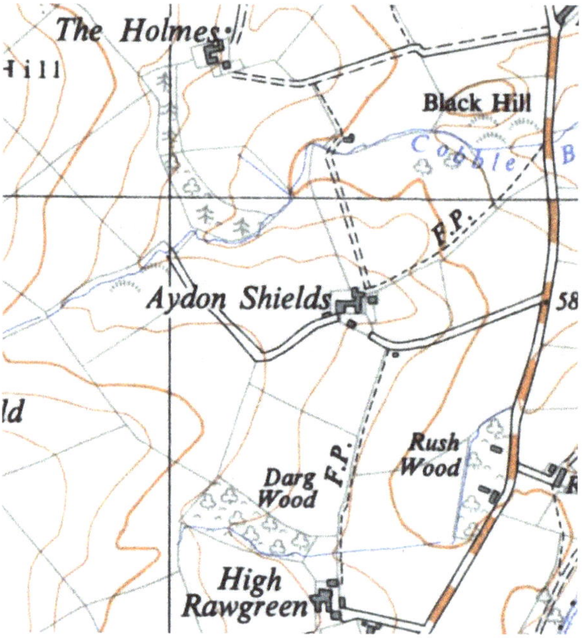

Fig 22: Aydon Shields farm on 'Hall hill' from which footpaths and trackways radiate in all directions (OS 1:25,000, 1968)

judge from the same 1735 map. At first glance it seems an odd location for such a hamlet: 900ft high (270m) and above the waterline, but it is one of the 'ley' placenames that lies on an outlier of better soil above the wet acid clay. LiDaR imagery of the narrow area containing a well on the 1735 map show hints of buildings that are possibly the remains of a once more populous settlement of four or more households at Rowley Head.[15] In 1608 Newbiggin Hill was let in quarters, suggesting a division into four original holdings, and Ordley was divided in the same way. In 1564 Dukesfield was said to have been '*late in the tenure of four men*'. Mollersteads was in three separate holdings.[16] Dalton was in at least four separate holdings as late as the 18th century. The 1839 tithe map shows the fossilised remnants of small farming strips to the south-west of the Lee either side of what had been a narrow band of common land until 1760.

This settlement pattern of small hamlets, informal clusters of steadings accompanied by a few arable strips, might therefore date from the period of early medieval colonisation, whether by independent settlers following the Devil's Water upstream, or through the agency of drengs from the 7th century. In the 'Werhale', land between the Tyne and Wear estuaries, Roberts suggested a colonisation pattern of hamlets such as these.[17] Unlike there, however, the Shire's small hamlets did not develop into larger villages. Ordley and the Lee are just half a mile apart but remained separate settlements.

Perhaps this pattern of small hamlets existed elsewhere in Northumberland in the transitional land between the fertile valleys and the high moorland, giving us an intermediate landscape of settlement between the stylised lowland and highland zones. This would be consistent with the 'infield outfield' system widespread in Northumberland before the modern era, where periodic small enclosures for temporary cropping on the higher ground – the 'outfield' – normally accompanied the intensively farmed strip field or fields. The thin fertility of the upland soils was soon exhausted, the hedges thrown down and the land reverted to the waste. Temporary cultivation of the outfield was still practised in the Shire as late as the mid-18th century.

The settlement pattern was also intermediate in that there were also many solitary farmsteads, to be expected in a landscape better suited to rearing livestock than raising crops. When later enclosures are stripped away from the map it's interesting to see how many of these steadings lay between their 'in ground' and the open fell, as illustrated in Figure 23. Further examples can be seen at Ardley, Hamburn Hall and Steel Hall. The current track from Dukesfield along to Steel Hall was the boundary – at about 600ft altitude (180m) – between the enclosed cultivated ground to the north and the waste at higher elevation to the south, the farmsteads lying between. Rough common grazing reduced pressure on lowland pastures especially when the growing season was short and grass quality poor. It allowed more of the better land to be kept free from stock and used as meadows – critical for the provision of winter feed. Direct access to the fells was therefore highly convenient. It meant those first settlers had less land to clear of wood, scrub and stones, and less to wall or fence. The value of this open grazing is illustrated at Steel Hall in the 1379 Black Book of Hexham Priory:

> *'They also have 1 sheepfold in Steel, at the west end, with 1 garden adjacent on the north side, containing 1 acre of land in total; and rights of common pasture for 300 sheep at all times of the year. And they have rights of common within all the bounds of Steel'.*[18]

Larger hamlets such as Ordley and Dotland also had direct access to the waste. The boundaries between waste and in-ground often tapered towards narrow openings to assist with funnelling stock back in to the byres and enclosed fields when necessary, as illustrated in Figures 23 and 37.

It is little more than surmise that the small hamlets described thus far were deliberate plantations, but this seems clearer at Dotland and Yarridge, which are shown as 'Later Estates?' on Figure 17. They are both

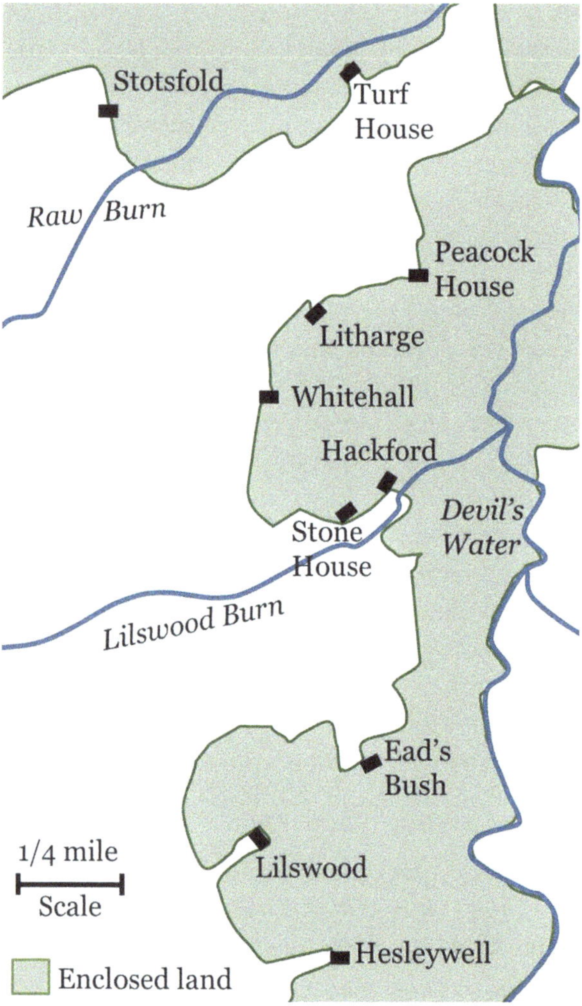

Fig 23: Location of farm steadings between ancient enclosed land and the waste in the High Quarter of Hexhamshire

located above the valleys, on outliers of light soil above the heavy clay, and were once divided into multiple tenements. Yarridge comprised six separate tenements – husbandlands – in 1379. Dotland was noticeably larger at 20 husbandlands and cottages in 1379, and it was possibly the largest single settlement in the Shire at the time. 'Dotta's land' appears to be one of the very few surviving Scandinavian personal placenames in the district.[19] This could date it as a late 9th or 10th century development, in the wake of the Viking invasions that disrupted the Northumbrian kingdom, followed in some places by settlement. Although on high ground at 750ft altitude (235m) there is a line of springs not far away. The earthworks marked as 'medieval village (site of)' on the OS map are easy to see on the ground, from the air and on LiDaR, but harder to interpret. However, in conjunction with 19th century maps they indicate the presence of two rows of buildings orientated roughly east-west either side of a green that narrows to the east, with a well to the upper and wider west end.

This is reminiscent of the layout of many planned villages that Brian Roberts feels were established in County Durham between the 10th and 12th centuries by the increasingly powerful landowning church in Durham.[20] It might therefore be significant that Hexhamshire, once part of St Wilfrid's domain, belonged to Durham by the start of the 11th century, perhaps earlier, before being transferred to the Archbishopric of York shortly after the Norman conquest.[21] Dotland was one of the early grants made by Archbishop Thurstan to the re-established Priory of Hexham between 1114 and 1140. It was described then as a 'vill' or township, which could imply either a settlement already in place, or a larger administrative area (which presumably included the later Dotland Park to the north-east) or both. Yarridge was possibly another such late-planned settlement, set into the waste on the high ridge once crossed by the Roman road. It too was a vill granted by the Archbishop to Hexham Priory, in around 1110. Dotland and Yarridge occupy similar sites above the valleys. Were they planned villages of the 10th or 11th centuries on the Durham pattern, breaking new higher ground as part of a deliberate policy of development, a policy continued by further land grants into the high medieval period under the Priory's ownership?[22] Although its later ownership history was different, Rowley Head's location potentially hints at similar origins to Yarridge and Dotland and it is therefore also denoted as a speculative 'Later Estate?' on Figure 17.

Another feature of the landscape revealed by the pre-enclosure map and placenames is transhumance. In upland areas suited to livestock farming pressure on the best grassland was eased in the summer by making use of rough pasture on the higher ground. In the North Tyne valley it was normal by medieval times for the entire community to move their herds and flocks to distant uplands together. Transhumance bears distant comparison with ancient patterns of seasonal migration from the time prehistoric hunters followed their prey to the high ground in summer. Those tending their cattle and sheep in the hills at a distance from their lowland home lived in huts between April and August. The Norse word for such huts gave rise to the '-scale' placename frequently found in the Lake District. The old English equivalent was 'shield'. Each lowland community's upland grazing land was known as its 'shieling' or summering grounds.

The current and known previous 'shield' placenames in the Shire are shown in Figure 24. They are mainly found on the broader areas of upland

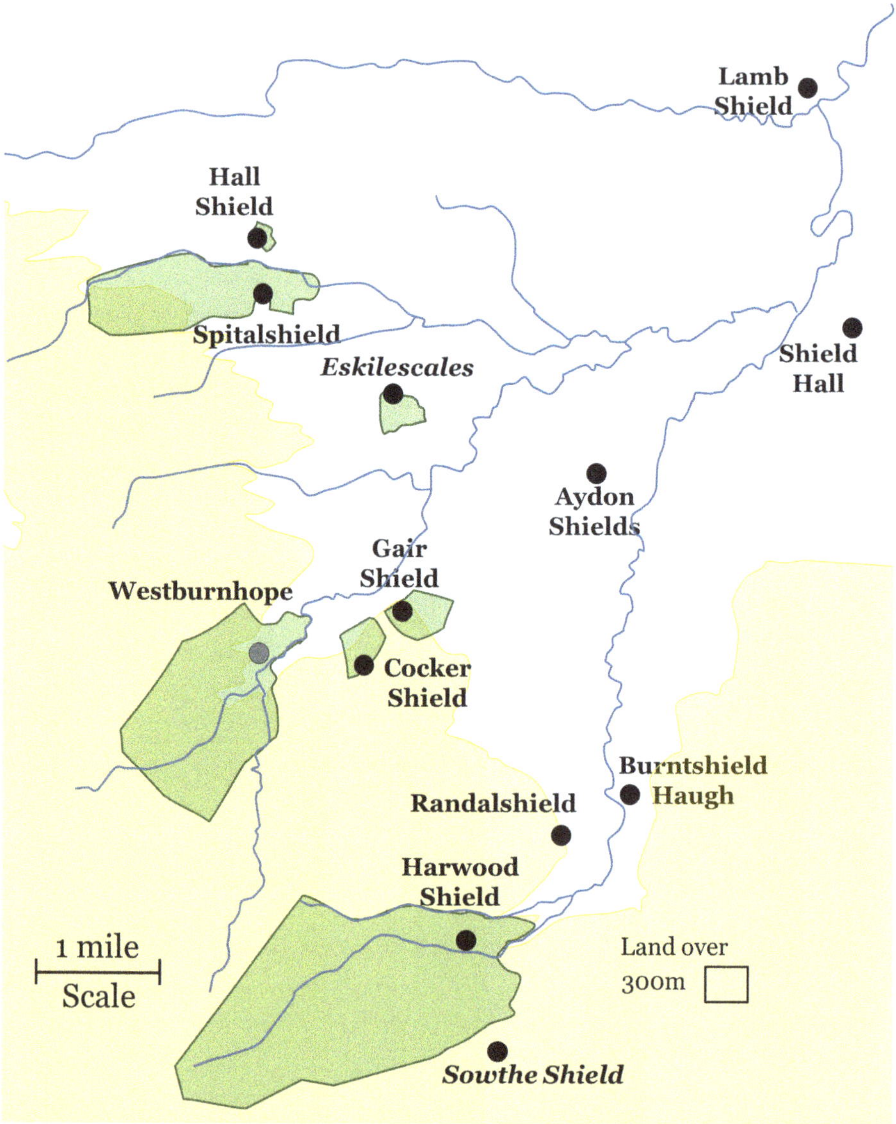

Fig 24: Shield placenames and potential large shieling grounds

to the west, although Aydon Shields, Shield Hall and Lamb Shield provide reminders that huts served other purposes. Those that can more confidently be linked to places elsewhere stand out more clearly as summering grounds. Spital Shield, for example, hints at an association with lowland grounds belonging to the Hospital of St Giles in Hexham, established through grants from the Archbishop of York, the manorial lord, possibly in the early 12th century.[23] Noticeably, Spital Shield has long had its own large area of enclosed moorland to the west. The whole 400 acres of the estate were recognised in the later Hexhamshire and Allendale Common Enclosure Award of 1800 as private land rather than common, and the same applied to Westburnhope (650 acres) and Harwood Shield (1,500 acres). All were owned by the Lord of the Manor until the 1660s or later. In 1404 *Harwood shele* 'being in the Forest of Nowland' [Newland] was part of Coastley sub-manor and estate, located at the foot of the Darden Burn west of Hexham, also owned by the Archbishop. Here too, surely, is a compelling link between the lowland farms around Coastley in the Tyne Valley and the western Shire uplands. Today's empty track southwards from Greenridge must have been alive with the migration of livestock, sheep and people each April and August. The large enclosed moorland pastures on high ground beyond the steadings of Spital Shield, Westburnhope and Harwood Shield might mark out the boundaries of medieval summering grounds let to lowland communities by the manorial lord.

Arable strip fields, meadows, lowland pasture and upland shielings were all key elements of the rural landscape taking shape in the early medieval Shire. Beyond them lay vast areas of moorland fell land. Although often described as 'waste', including elsewhere in this book, the upland commons were crucial in providing roofing thatch from heather or ling, peat fuel, and occasional small game for food, in addition to summer grazing.

Fig 25: The smallholding of Ardley Stobb, now in ruins. Its name probably signifies old wood pasture, which fits with its location above the Ham Burn on what was common land until the 18th century.

Thin slabs of the mudstone found amidst the sedimentary rocks in the cleughs made good stones on which to bake the dietary staple of oatcakes, such as at Backstone Cleugh above Westburnhope. Much woodland also remained, particularly on the steep banks of the burns threading their way towards Corbridge. Although land was cleared of trees for cultivation, woodland remained of agricultural importance as well as for building material. Trees that had reached beyond the browsing height of cattle were subsequently pruned – pollarded – to exploit new growth and to allow enough light to reach the ground to support grass. Such wood pasture was part of the landscape for centuries, and is today often indicated by the presence of old pollards, some given away by hollowed-out trunks, and the 'stobb' placename element.

Some land in the south of the Shire was designated as 'forest'. This was a legal term for reserved hunting ground, rather than necessarily woodland. Strictly speaking 'forest' was royal hunting ground, but since the great medieval landowner in the Shire was a churchman, the Archbishop of York, the ground would more accurately have been a 'chase'. We cannot be sure exactly where this was but a 1233 charter mentioned the 'foresta de Lillswude', and the 'Forest of Nowland' mentioned above can be identified

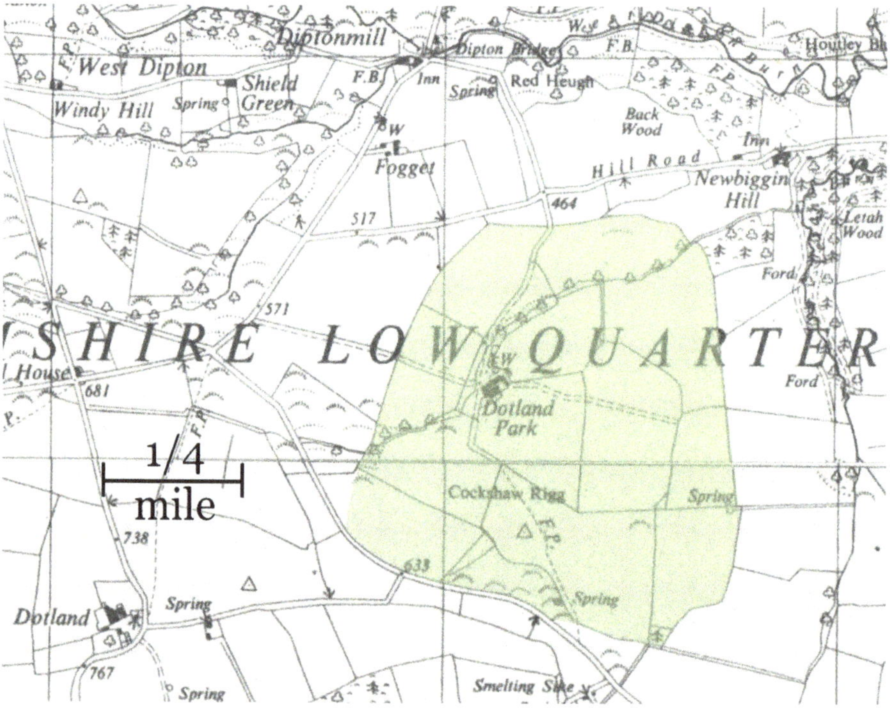

Fig 26: Hexham Priory's medieval hunting ground at Dotland Park (OS base, 2.5in, 1950)

Fig 27 (right): Late 15th/ early 16th century gable end of Dotland Park, the Prior's hunting lodge
Fig 28 (below): The curved boundary of the medieval Lillswood Park 'forest' is clearly revealed from the air, here viewed from the north-west.

with much the same area. The name Lillswood Park hints at forest land fenced or walled off into a park, suitable for hunting deer. The graceful rounded boundary wall of Lillswood Farm looks very much like a deer park's boundary (see Figure 28). A similar pattern can be seen around Dotland Park, which was Hexham Priory's hunting estate by 1296. Since the Archbishop had one, the Prior doubtless also felt he deserved his own (see Figures 26-27). The Lillswood/Newlands forest possibly ran right over

Hope Fell and Blackburn Head to join up with a forest on the Blanchland side of the fell, for in the mid-16th century the forester in charge of each seems to have been the same man, George Ord.[24] The Archbishop's forest could therefore have covered a large area of the upper Devil's Water valley, but it's important to note that livestock grazing was often permitted over the forest land, for a fee or in return for labour service, and it helped to keep the gallops clear. Just such a tenancy given for labour service was the land at the site of Five Dykes today, anciently Five Dargue, or Five Days Work. It was almost certainly within Lillswood Park.

Although it is likely that independent settlement, drengage, and transhumance were the key factors that brought about the recolonization of Hexhamshire's land in the early to high medieval period, it is probably impossible to determine their sequence. We might, however, suggest that Yarridge, Dotland and – more speculatively – Rowley Head were planned as later villages under the auspices of Durham at some point from the 10th century because much of the better land at lower altitudes around them was already settled and farmed. The climate had been improving again from around the ninth century AD and by the late 1200s was warmer than at any time since the Bronze Age. As elsewhere, the high medieval period of the 12th and 13th centuries witnessed great economic expansion. Much land was reclaimed for agriculture, presumably under an increasing pressure of population. We are able to trace some of this in the surviving documentary record. Many land grants are of assarts – clearances from the waste, including several from the 1220s showing how Dotland's cultivated land spread southwards and eastwards from the hilltop settlement. One of these grants, in 1226, talked of assarts 'already made and those which shall be made in future', betraying a clear assumption that the clearance process had momentum and would continue.[25] Dotland was almost certainly the largest settlement in the Shire, with 20 households or more by the end of the 13th century. The distinctive hedgebank of one of Dotland's medieval open fields can still be seen inside the field gate on the west side of the road between Dotland and Channel Well today, and another, that of the south field, east of the road up from Barker House (see Figure 29). Elsewhere, 64 acres were granted by Archbishop Gray of York at Hamburn Hall in the 1220s and 1230s.

Further south, the Lillswood area also attracted the name of Newland at some time between 1233 and 1404, which sounds like newly reclaimed land. As mentioned above, much of this was a hunting forest but there was a still a grant of 60 acres in Lillswood 'on the Devil's Water' – possibly Lillswood Park – on condition that it was 'reduced to cultivation'.

Figs 29 and 30: The medieval bank of Dotland South Field, looking east *(above)*, and curved walls at the Foggett, possible remains of a high medieval assart from the waste

The same distinctive bulbous pattern resulting from the backbreaking work of reclaiming land from the fell can be seen in the area – not just around Lillswood (deer park or not) but also uphill from Stonehouse, Whitehall and Litharge – Little Ridge. The steadings thus 'reduced to cultivation' during the great medieval expansion all have their small inbye fields, direct access to the fell, a burn or spring nearby and perhaps some adjacent wood pasture. Many of these curved wall lines of piecemeal assarting or clearance have since been straightened out, but a fine example remains at the Foggett, up the hill south of Dipton Mill, a lovely graceful wall between the modern bungalow and the old Foggett fields beyond (Figure 30).

The intensification of land use during the medieval period is also seen in the conversion of shielings into permanently settled farms. Randalshield, not far south of Lilswood, became 'New House' at some point. The Eshells was first set down in writing in the late 12th and early 13th centuries as *Eskeinggeseles* and *Eskilescales*, the latter form hinting at a rare local instance of the Norse 'scale' name element. By 1226 the men of Eshells were expected to take their corn to Whitley Mill, hinting that the land was then in permanent occupation. Crops were evidently by then being grown 850ft (260m) up on the heavy clay.[26]

Whitley Mill was one of two corn mills operating in the Shire from the 13th century. Its mill race can still be seen from the road bridge south of Dalton, snaking away over the field to the east, 'Abbey Holm', a slightly inaccurate recognition of the mill's original construction for the Priory. The other mill was at Newbiggin, not far from good cropland at Ordley, and on the way towards Hexham's market. The town was presumably also an expanding market for the many industrial raw materials produced in pastoral landscapes, including cow hides, sheep skins and wool. Barker House possibly owes its name to the practice of gathering bark, important to leather-making. An increasingly commercial – as opposed to feudal – economy can be surmised by the evidence that half of the Priory's tenants at Dotland occupied cottages with plots of land too small to provide subsistence – they presumably laboured for others. Medieval prosperity is also indicated by the survival to this day of buildings from that period – notably the tower house at Shield Hall with walls so thick a spiral staircase can run up inside one of them.

The strain of population growth and economic expansion by the end of the 13th century is illustrated by the survival of medieval rigg and furrow on high and poor ground that has not been ploughed since. Google Earth and LiDaR reveal an extensive area at Winnowty Hill on the windswept ground west of Greenridge at 790ft altitude (240m). A similar pattern shows up

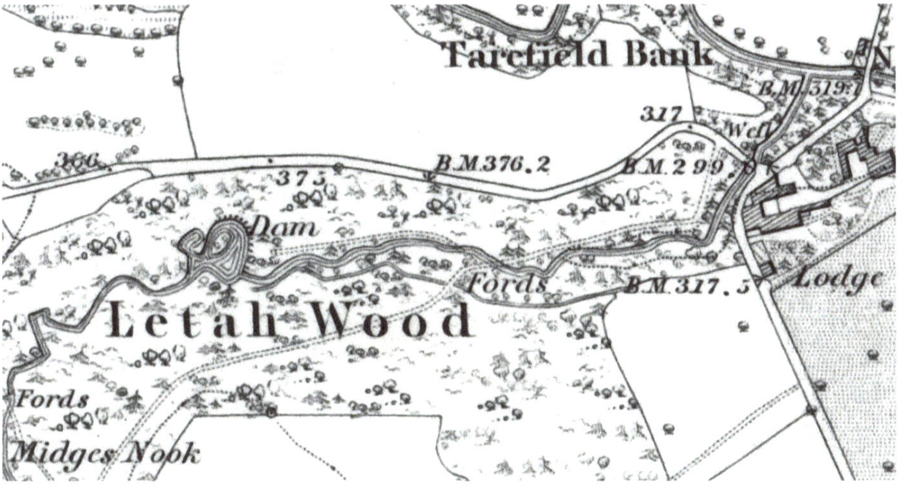

Figs 31 and 32: The Newbiggin mill race, probably originating in the high medieval period, ran eastwards through Letah Woods from the dam shown in the 1860 OS map, and its remains can be seen in the woods today.

just south-west of Salmonfield, and to the immediate north of Spital Shield, as shown in Figure 33: some 50 acres or so of sinuous wide rigg and furrow on the north-facing clay rising to 950ft high (290m). It looks very much like the subtle remains of arable land pushed to the margin of cultivation under pressure of 13th century population growth.

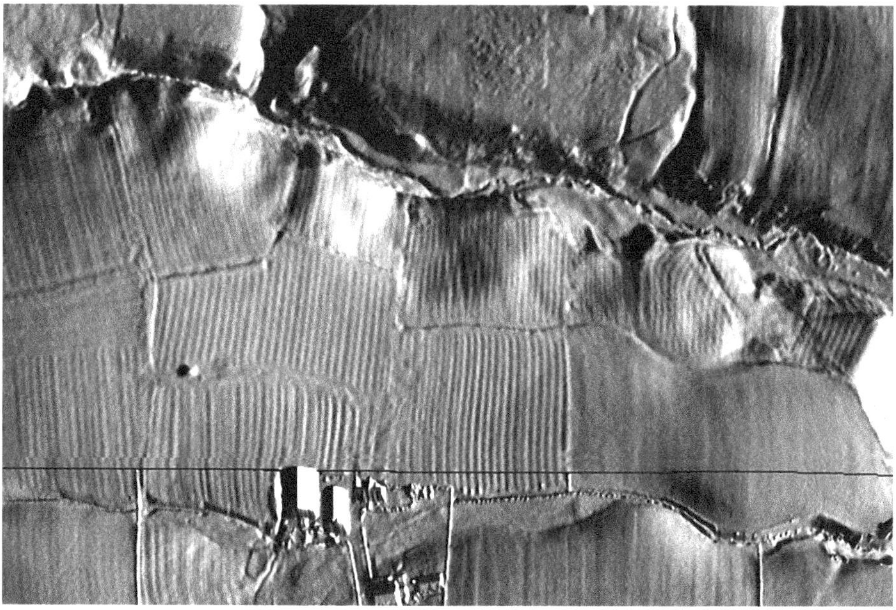

Fig 33: LiDaR image of medieval rig and furrow at Spital Shield

A major reversal came at the end of the 13th century, heralded by the onset of the Scottish Wars from 1296 and the burning of Hexham Priory. The pendulum of climatic change was also swinging back again bringing deteriorating conditions. For a growing society that had pushed its resources to the limit a few wet and cold summers between 1315-7 spelt disaster. Famine was followed by livestock epidemics into the 1320s, all revealed by petitions from the Priory in 1328, and two decades later came the first of several devastating waves of bubonic plague. The Priory's hunting lodge at Dotland Park was improved, and the walls raised in 1354, perhaps to create what the Prior thought would provide a safe haven away from the pestilence down in the town.

Ebb: the Black Death

We get glimpses of the profound impact of the Black Death in the 'Black Book', a detailed listing of the Priory's property drawn up in 1379. The 20 earlier farm tenements and cottages at Dotland were by 1379 occupied by just six tenants. Only Whitley Mill was still in operation, Newbiggin being presumably surplus to requirements at a time when the shortage of labour and deteriorating weather conditions were contributing factors in a shift from arable towards pastoral farming. It feels safe to assume that much of the land broken in for ploughing at the peak of the medieval boom was abandoned during the 14th century. Broad ridges and gentle reversed

'S' curves survive where the land has not been worth ploughing since. Before the Black Death Hexham Priory collected their corn tithes into a large barn 'at the east end of the vill of Rowley' (which might cautiously be located at the Steel), but this was in a ruinous state by 1379. And this wasn't the end of it. Whitley Mill provided over £4 of rent to the Priory in 1379, but by 1547 this had been reduced to little more than a quarter of that level, presumably reflecting the reduction in the amount of corn to be ground and a smaller population. The deep zig-zagged hollow way running northwards down to the mill from Whitley crossroads must have carried less traffic after the high medieval period.

A great shortage of labour following the Black Death changed the balance of economic power. The 15th century has been called the 'golden age of the labourer'. Sheer scarcity of manpower meant far more opportunities for the enterprising and the independent to improve their lot than hitherto and many of the institutions and obligations of high feudalism gave way. Those six tenants left at Dotland had evidently accumulated larger land holdings and there were still six, rather than the previous 20, by 1536.[27] If Aydon Shields was a small hamlet in earlier medieval times, by 1527 it had been consolidated into a single farm on its small hill. It's hard to imagine that Rowley Head remained under the plough in such times.

The shifting balance of power from landlord to tenant was reflected in the 'terms and conditions' of their customary tenancies. The vast majority of tenants in Hexhamshire held their land 'by copy of the manor court roll', and were therefore known as copyholders. The authorities had a strong incentive to keep the border areas well populated, to provide a body of men available for military service against the Scots and defend against reivers. This inevitably meant easing rent burdens. Any such relaxation was effectively locked in. Rents and entry fines – payable when the holding was transferred – were fixed at levels that, while possibly onerous in medieval times, were beneficial to tenants as prices rose from the 16th century. In 1535 the total rent due from Dotland was the same as in 1379, shortly after the Black Death. And by then a recovery was underway. A guess at the population of the Shire at its medieval peak, and it can only be a guess, based on known hamlets and farms and making an allowance for the landless, would be perhaps 480-500 people. If this fell at between by up to a half as elsewhere, then by 1400 there would have been perhaps only 250-280 or so people left. An estimate from the 1538 muster roll, as the medieval world gave way to the early modern, suggests the Shire population had risen to between 330 and 380 by then. Copyholders were well placed to benefit from changed economic fortunes.

As the Warden of the Middle March (charged with keeping the Scots at bay) noted glumly to London in 1580, when reviewing a poor turnout at the muster, there were

> *'six score copyholders in Hexhamshire, bound by their 'copies' to find horse & armour, who 'taverne their land' [effectively sub-letting it to others] and give it at will as if they were freeholders. As the steward and officers cannot remedy this without a special commission, the Lord Treasurer is prayed to issue the same'.*[28]

A survey of the 'Newlands and Rowley Ward' of Hexham Manor in 1547, (ie. the Shire) shows exactly this process at work, and that a few people now held several of the copyholds.[29] Thomas Armstrong at Ordley, Richard Thirlwall at Newbiggin and Ardley, John Swinburne at Black Hall, Steel, Dalton, Barkerhouse and Mollersteads, and the Hurdes or Ords, the foresters in the Lillswood area, had all been able to build up clusters of copyholds. With population and economic recovery underway in a new era, and prices rising, the true value of the land began to outstrip the fixed rents, and these energetic copyholders were the beneficiaries.

[1] Summarised in M Adams, *The First Kingdom*, (2021).
[2] T Williamson, Environment, *Society and Landscape in Early Medieval England*, (2013), pp.44-5; P Sarris, 'New Approaches to the 'Plague of Justinian', *Past & Present*, 254, (2022), pp.315-46.
[3] Green and Finch, *op cit*, pp.45-6.
[4] T Corfe, 'The Battle of Heavenfield', *HH*, 7, (1997), p.73.
[5] B K Roberts, 'Time & Tide in North East England', in W Lancaster, D Newton & N Vall (eds), *An Agenda For Regional History*, (2007).
[6] Allendale Estate collection; an extract is shown in Figure 38.
[7] C O'Brien, 'The Early Medieval Shires of Yeavering, Breamish and Bamburgh', *AA*, 5th ser, 30, (2002); B Roberts, 'Northumberland: reflections on prehistoric, Roman and Old English settlement', *AA*, 5th ser, 44, (2015).
[8] HN-6, p.180.
[9] C O'Brien & M Adams, 'The Identification of Early Medieval Monastic Estates in Northumbria', *Medieval Settlement Research*, (2016), p.26. There was seemingly also an early monastic settlement at Bywell.
[10] V Watts, The Place-Name Hexham', *HH*, 5, (1995), pp.4-5.
[11] HN-3, pp. 31-4, 66-86. There were 12, including Hexham town. Several early medieval small shires often included 12 drengages.
[12] E Miller, 'Northern England', H Hallam (ed) *Agricultural History of England and Wales, II, 1042-1350* (1988) p.407.
[13] Mawer speculated that its name, first recorded as Aldenscheles in the 14th century, derived from the English personal name Ealdwine. Perhaps he was the dreng. A Mawer, *The Place-names of Northumberland and Durham*, (1920).
[14] TNA MPII/1/40/3.
[15] AVH, Appendix 4–features 90561&2 'farmstead and earthwork', p.99.
[16] HN-3, pp.90-91; NRO 2762/DEEDS.
[17] B K Roberts, 'The Land of Werhale - Landscapes of Bede' *AA*, 5th ser, 37, (2008).
[18] Black Book, p.75. As it is listed alongside other holdings of the Priory in '*Sclavelye*' (ie. Slaley) it must refer to the present day Steel Hall rather than the Steel, on the other side of the Devil's Water.
[19] Mawer, *place-names, op cit*.
[20] B K Roberts, *Landscapes, Documents and Maps*, (2008).
[21] D Rollason, 'Hexham after the Vikings', *HH*, 5, (1995), pp.6-16.
[22] Black Book, pp. 247, 269-70.
[23] D Gardner-Medwin, 'The Hospital of St.Giles at Hexham', *HH*, 13 (2003), pp.4-5. 'The Spital' is today the site of Hexham golf club, west of the town.
[24] Dotland Park: Black Book, p.247; Lillswood: HN-3, pp. 31-4, p.76.
[25] Black Book, p.189.
[26] Mawer, *Place Names*; Black Book, p.249.
[27] Black Book, p.171.
[28] J Bain (ed), *Calendar of Border Papers*, (1894), Vol.1, p.22.
[29] HN-3, pp. 66-86.

4. The early modern flowing tide

Fig 34: Illustrative reconstruction of the phased extension of Wester Steel in the early modern period

The confidence of the rising class of copyholders accumulating land in the mid-16th century is seen in the evidence of new building. One of George Orde's farmholdings in 1547 was 'Stanehouse', near Hackford, a term of pride and distinction in days when to build in stone instead of turf was a status symbol (see Figure 35). There was also a stonehouse at Dukesfield by 1564. When Wester Steel was renovated in the 1990s it was carefully examined by Peter Ryder, and the earliest section was tentatively dated to the mid/late-16th century (Figure 34).[1] These stone houses pre-date the building of bastles around the end of the 16th century, a number of which also survive in the Shire: for example at High Holms, Stobby Lea and Hesleywell (see Figure 36). These three have doors in the middle of the range, rather than in the gable ends as seen elsewhere in Northumberland, so possibly adjoined other structures. Bastle houses are often used to portray a desolate and lawless period in Northumberland, underwritten by fearful contemporary accounts dispatched to London by royal officials seeking more money and men. While acknowledging the raiding and feuding in the thinly populated border valleys and hills north of the Tyne, the construction of new mills in the later 16th century in Hexhamshire suggests a measure of stability, even quiet prosperity. Bastles were indeed defensive structures, but could only be built by people with resources – and who felt they had wealth worth protecting. This is worth bearing in mind when considering their crude but sturdy form and their quiet longevity.

Fig 35 (top): Stonehouse near Hackford. *Fig 36 (above):* Hesleywell Bastle

A survey of Hexham manor in 1608 for the Crown provides other evidence of economic recovery in earlier decades. Copyholder independence was clearly still resented by the royal surveyors, and they in turn were hardly welcome visitors. In a closing note they said:

> *'All the copihoulde and custumarie tenantes ther clayme their lands as copiholders of inheritance to them, their heris and assignes, according to the custome, for rent, fine and border service. Their fines they pretende to be certaine. ... They have ther, for certaine, verie ancient evidences and courtrolls, but they would not showe them unto us, nor any of their coppies'.*[2]

The surveyors set down their view as to the true value of each tenancy next to the actual rent paid (which had not increased since 1547). By 1608 the land was estimated to be worth six to seven times as much. No wonder the crown wanted to change such secure tenancies to leases, which was happening all along the border following the Union of the Crowns. However, when this was tried in 1610 in Hexhamshire it was overturned in the Court of Exchequer, presumably to much rejoicing by the copyholders. Peter Ryder dated the second phase of building at the Steel to the early 17th century, and it might therefore reflect this legal confirmation of the copyholder's security of tenure. Erstwhile tenants of the manorial lord were bold enough to buy their freeholds – Henry Johnson, William Winter and William Pearson doing so respectively at Hamburn Hall, Spital Shield and Harwood Shield, buying from the financially weakened Fenwick family, inheritors of the old Archbishopric of York's estate, in the 1660s and 1670s.[3]

The region as a whole was beginning to develop under the influence of the Newcastle coal trade from the 1570s, which generated demand for food and industrial materials from the port's hinterland. Hexham, on a natural transport route to Tyneside just below the junction of the North and South Tyne, was a good market location between upland and lowland districts for supplying the needs of Newcastle. The Shire's proximity to Hexham must have meant an increase in demand for meat, dairy produce, hides and wool from the cattle and sheep to which the land was best suited. In 1620 Cocker Shield and Riddlehamhope (alias Sowthe Shiel), both over 1,000ft high (300m), were described as newly built tenements – a date that ties in with possible 'bastle' footings at Riddlehamhope. Both were given over to large sheep flocks.[4] Several small enclosures or folds can be seen near streams in the hills, and often the name 'Washpool', where sheep were washed in summer. Washpool hill is near Westburnhope and Lady's Washpool was on common land on the Rowley Burn south of Dalton.

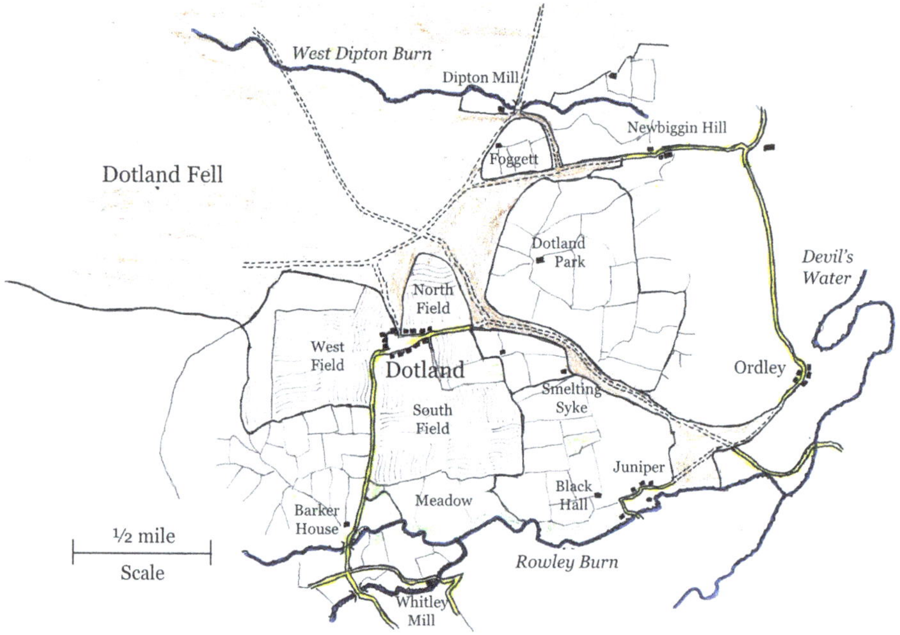

Fig 37: 17th century Dotland, reconstructed from documentary and field evidence

The demands on farming, especially the pressure of pastoral farming on good grassland, affected the landscape in two broad ways during this period. Firstly, many of the strips of arable cultivation within the scattered small open fields around the Shire's hamlets were enclosed into individual fields. They probably already accounted for no more than a small fraction of the cultivated land. Dotland's fields were surely the largest, having three fields of perhaps 100 acres each to the south, west and north (see Figure 37). Dalton's open fields can't have comprised more than 100 acres in total, Aydon Shield and Rawgreen's around 80 acres each and no more than this at The Steel. However, because the strips were rotated between oats, bigg (a type of barley) and fallow by communal agreement it was difficult to turn more of them to permanent grass, despite attractive prices for pastoral produce, without removing them altogether.

Under the old system, individual riggs might be fenced off temporarily, using stakes interwoven with cut brushwood – dry hedges – but these were never very strong, and many are the complaints in manor court records of people leaving their dry hedges in a poor state of repair. In 1683, for example, Richard Teasdell of Dotland's hedges were '*very much out of repair to the great damage of his neighbours*'.[5] Upon permanent enclosure dry hedges were replaced with 'live' hedges, planted to grow permanently stock-proof. No longer did all the land have to follow the old arable rotations. More land overall was laid to grass. The need for long distance upland summering dwindled. Selective stock rearing also became easier for individual farmers to pursue, and rams could be kept physically separate from the ewes until tupping time at the end of October. No-one wanted lambs until late spring when the new grass grew.

Enclosure was far easier to accomplish if the land was held by a small number of farmers, preferably just one. A 1631 lease at Aydon Shields shows that its old strips were enclosed by then. Yarridge was farmed by a single tenant by 1635 and, in all probability, enclosed. Dotland and Dalton's common fields took longer to enclose for the land was held by different copyholders until the early 18th century. The Rowland family at Dotland painstakingly went about buying up the many separate copyholds there over many decades in the late 17th century, and the open fields were not enclosed until 1714. Separate holdings at Dalton were bought by Christopher Teasdale in the 1730s and so probably lay open until then.[6] Thus were the Shire's remaining small open arable fields enclosed in a piecemeal fashion, more of it to be used as permanent pasture rather than ploughed and sown with grain. Although one or two riggs remained open at Turf House until at least 1800, they were probably by then an isolated relic from earlier days (see Figure 21).[7]

Crops, mainly oats, continued to be grown for a few years at a time on the uplands in small temporary outfields until the soil was exhausted of nutrients. Corn was grown on intakes as high as 1,300ft (400m) up on the flanks of Pikeley Rigg near Harwood Shield in the 1690s. In 1662 Sir William Fenwick, as Lord of the Manor, gave £3 per year out of intake rents or 'acre money' to help pay for a schoolmaster at Whitley Chapel. At the going rate per acre this implies some 180 acres at a time – a tiny amount in the context of over 20,000 acres of unenclosed moorland.[8] Land above Embley was still taken in for temporary intakes in the 1750s. North and west of Edge House several tilled fields of between 3 and 20 acres in size can be seen on LiDaR images of the rough pasture and open common at 950ft altitude (290m) on Greenrigg Moor, many of the ridges and boundaries still visible on the ground. Some are relics of isolated single fields; others share boundaries with each other. Similar sized irregular ploughed intakes underlie later enclosures west of Eshells at 300m altitude (see Figure 39). Some were only ever temporary, but others became permanent enclosures of cultivated land or improved pasture taken from the common. A map of Nubbock and Paise Common from the early 1770s shows a series of fields of between four and 20 acres labelled 'incroachments' to the west of '*West Greenridge Antient Ground*' (Figure 38). Beyond it were other fields taken

Fig 38: 'Incroachments' from West Greenridge onto the common, c.1770

in from the fell, the 'incroachments' of Low Stublock, Payes and Nubbock. The surveyors reported that while the land in question had only ever been allowed as temporary outfield for cultivation, it was now permanently fenced in from the waste.[9]

Here is a glimpse of the second main way in which farming was expanded and extended: the piecemeal permanent enclosure of land from the vast open fell land. Several farms in the Shire were surveyed in 1792 to identify encroachments onto the commons ahead of the Parliamentary enclosure of the Hexhamshire and Allendale Common. A complete set survive for the Eshells area and they can be pieced together to indicate how much land had been fenced in from the common by then (see Figure 39). Since they appear to lie above small temporary intakes visible on LiDaR to the west, of eight to 15 acres in size, they possibly date from the 18th century. Taking High and Low Eshells, the Heigh, Winter House and Hamburn Hall together, the earlier islands of in-bye land comprised about 450 acres of 'ancient enclosure'. By 1792 a further 210 acres had been taken in from the common, an increase of 44%. The new enclosures were generally large and irregular in shape, suggesting pastoral rather than arable use.

Another example of encroachment can be found in the Devil's Water

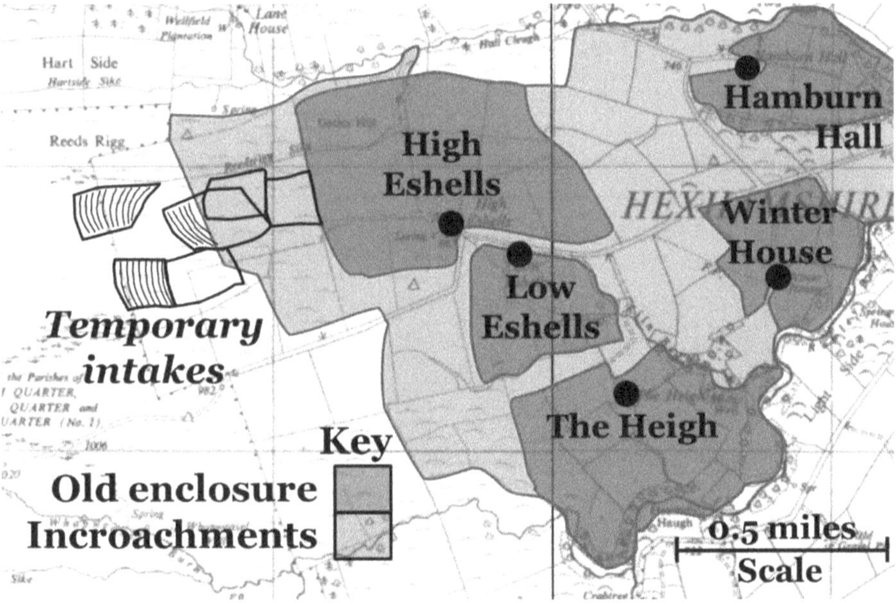

Fig 39: Temporary intakes and encroachments in the Eshells area (OS base 2.5in, 1950)

valley, to the south of the track between Dukesfield and Steel Hall. The fields there were identified separately from the 'ancient land' to the north of the track on a 1771 map drawn up as part of the Bulbeck Common enclosure work. Between 1659 and 1687 Richard Farelamb of Steel Hall was

> *'desirous to take away the barrenness and unfruitfulness of the said lands ... [He] did cause them to be digged, turned over and ploughed, and the heath, hather, ling and great stones, with axes, hatchets and spades did cause to be cut up, extirpated and rooted, and the same lands, by paring, burning, ploughing, and manuring, did convert from their former barrenness and unfruitfulness into arable land'.*[10]

A map of Aydon Shields drawn up in 1735 for the Greenwich Hospital shows areas of 'improved' land that had been extended from the medieval core. This was not high quality land. As late as 1774 the large open area of the Haggs (enclosed by 1631) was described as 'over-run with bushes & underwood' so was probably used only as rough pasture. But it was secured to Aydon Shield alone and relieved pressure on the precious meadowland at a time when pastoral farming was becoming more important (see Figure 60).

Thus was the Shire's landscape changing between the 16th and 18th centuries in response to the pressures and opportunities of economic specialisation. London drove the coal trade, and Newcastle's consequent growth created demands that rippled outwards into Tynedale. Hexham's population grew significantly, and so did the Shire's. As mentioned above, in the 1530s the Shire population might have been between 330 and 380 people. In the 1670s it was around 650, representing growth that matched or even exceeded the national rate between the same dates.[11] Dotland, so hard hit by the Black Death, had recovered to number around 20 households again by the 1680s, probably similar to its high medieval level.[12] The dilapidated chapel of St Helen was rebuilt in the 1650s as a community effort, led by William Rowland of Dotland Park. He was a substantial copyholder confident enough of his position to extract timbers and financial contributions from the Lord of the Manor Sir William Fenwick and Sir Edward Ratcliffe of Dilston.[13] Land was being taken in from the waste, with or without permission. All this took place during the significant climatic deterioration of the 'little ice age', when the Thames froze. From pre-history through to the medieval period, the frontier of farming tended to expand and contract with climatic cycles. In the century or two before the Industrial Revolution, however, the Shire's rural economy was breaking loose from some of its environmental moorings and expanding rather than contracting.

Fig 40: St Helen's church, Whitley Chapel, rebuilt in the 1740s

[1] P Ryder, 'A House in Hexhamshire: Recent Investigations of the Tenement, Steel', *HH*, 10 (2000).
[2] HN-3, p.104.
[3] Hamburn Hall and Spital Shield: NRO 4532/1-2. Harwood Shield: I Hancock, 'The Irish Gent and his strumpet: the story of Hercules Burleigh', *HH* 22 (2012), p.38.
[4] DUL CLV/f.420. At Riddlehamhope this might have been a rebuilding, as it was in existence in the 14th century: HN-4, p.70.
[5] Anick Grange Manor Court, 1683: NRO 672/A/16/43.
[6] G Finch, 'Dotland Deserted', *HH* 18 (2008); deeds in private collection.
[7] Turf House map: TNA ADM 66/85.
[8] TNA C 10/346/10; G.Ritschel, *An Account of Certain Charities*, (1713), p.10; DUL CLV f416.
[9] NRO 672/A/34/22.
[10] Map in a private collection; HN-6, p.383.
[11] Hearth Tax assessments and exemptions TNA E179/158/110, E179/340.
[12] Finch, Dotland, *op cit*, p.34. Dotland's population does appear to have fallen again significantly in the early 18th century, probably at around the time of the enclosure of its open fields, but at least some of the former inhabitants remained nearby.
[13] *ibid*. The church was rebuilt again in the 1740s.

5. Industry, trade and traffic

Closer integration of the English economy meant more trade and therefore more traffic. Locally, a great deal more produce must have been carried into Hexham. As far as we know, the first two road bridges in the Shire were built in the early modern period and they both lay on routes into Hexham. Neither the Linnels or Dipton roads were bridged in 1552, but the old stone on Linnels bridge bears the date 1581 and the Dipton Burn was bridged no later than the 1660s, and possibly much earlier. Most routes through the Shire ran across unenclosed land and traffic presumably meandered around the worst mud, ruts and other obstructions, but at Rawgreen and further north at Dalton the track – or lonnen – to Hexham between the enclosed grounds narrowed noticeably. Poor road conditions at these pinch points were certainly brought to the manor court's attention:

'at Dalton Loaning is a high way and the parish ought to maintaine it. It is to be sufficiently repaired at or before ye first of May next. Likewise we find that ye Rawgreene Loaning is out of repaire... We order yt shal be repaired and made sufficient before May day next or parish to be fined 40s [shillings, ie. £2].' [1]

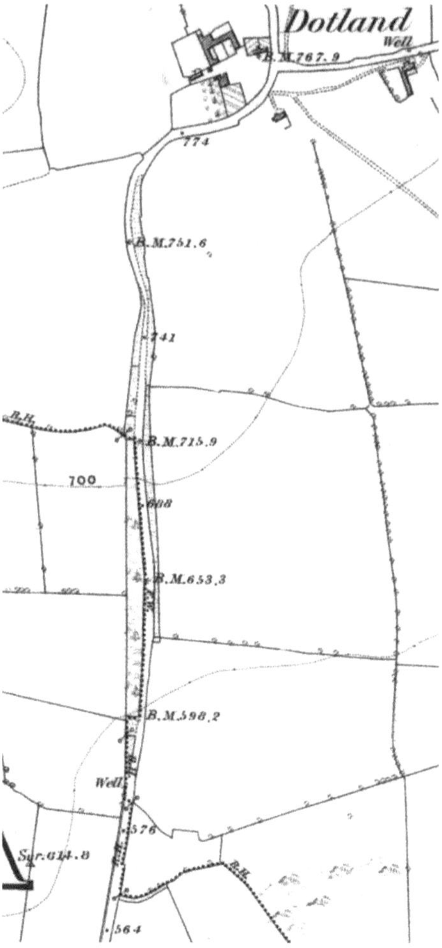

Fig 41: North of Barker House the roadway climbed up to Dotland between enclosed fields. The roadway between the old hedges, still visible beyond today's verges, widens from 10 metres to 30 metres on the steepest part of the ascent, giving more room for traffic to find ways around the worst patches, or to 'zig-zag' and thereby reduce the gradient of ascent. The Simpson family, blacksmiths at Dotland for several generations from at least the 1660s, were well-placed for traffic along this route, as were the smithies further south at Dalton crossroads and at Turf House (OS 6in, 1860).

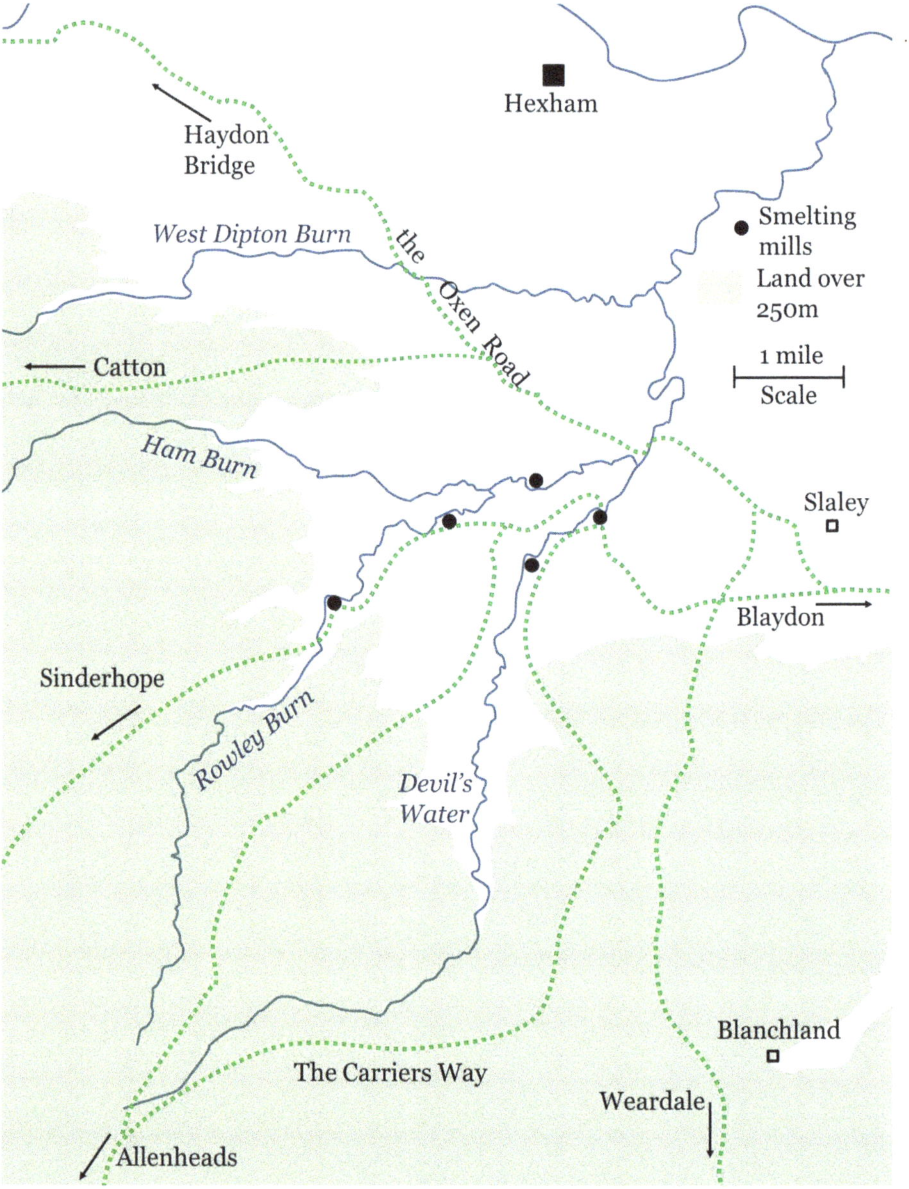

Fig 42: Principal trackways through Hexhamshire in the 17th and 18th century, including those used for cattle droving and for the carriage of lead ore from the south-west and of smelted lead eastwards towards Tyneside

Longer distance routes also crossed the Shire. Cattle and sheep were driven on foot from Scotland and Northumberland to London in increasing numbers in the 17th and 18th centuries. From Stagshaw Bank a droving road crossed the Tyne at Corbridge and climbed to the unenclosed ridge on the eastern watershed of the Devil's Water above Wooley and Shield

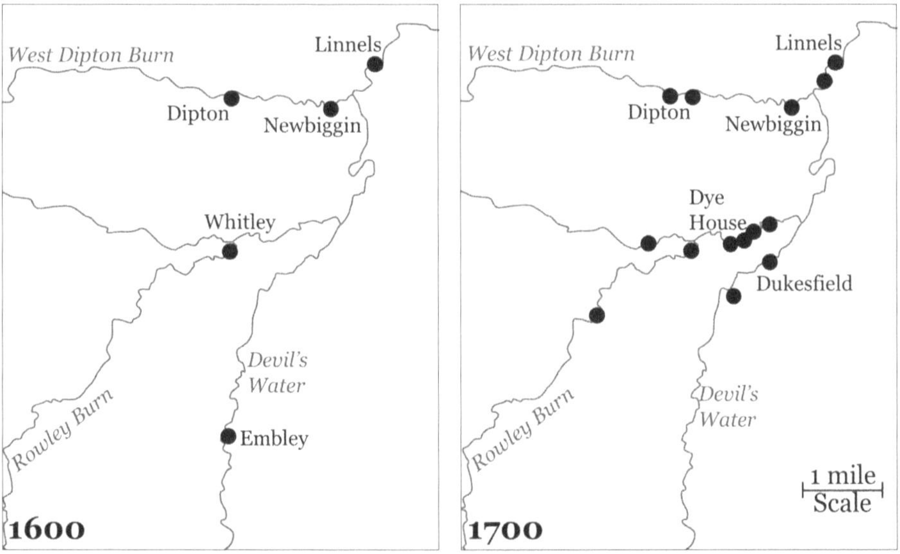

Fig 43: Watermills in 1600 and 1700. Selected names given for orientation

Hall. At Spring House there was a resting place, a stance, for the cattle before climbing the hill southwards over Dukesfield Fell and Blanchland Moor. The 'oxen road' joined this route near Shield Hall, having come from the north-west direction from the Northumberland fells to cross the Tyne at Haydon Bridge. It dropped down from the present racecourse ridge just west of Yarridge, crossed the Dipton Burn below Windy Hill, and then wound through the corridor of open common between Dotland and Dotland Park to the Peth, and thence up to Shield Hall. Oxenrods, Smelting Syke, and the Traveller's Rest were all pubs on this route, effectively a Hexham bypass for long distance cattle and sheep traffic (see Figure 42).

However from the 16th to the 18th centuries more was going on in the Shire than growing or raising more agricultural produce for distant markets or witnessing long distance traffic passing through. Industry flourished too. A large increase in the number of active mills gives a good indication of this. Youthful streams on relatively steep gradients meant that only relatively short and therefore inexpensive mill races or leats were needed to achieve a decent head of water onto mill wheels (see Figure 44). The flat outcrops of hard sandstone of the underlying sedimentary geology provided good foundations in the river beds for the weirs needed to divert water into the leats. Only Whitley Mill was active at the end of the medieval period, but by 1600 the number of mills had risen to at least five. This 16th century expansion is hardly consistent with claims that it was backward, lawless border country.

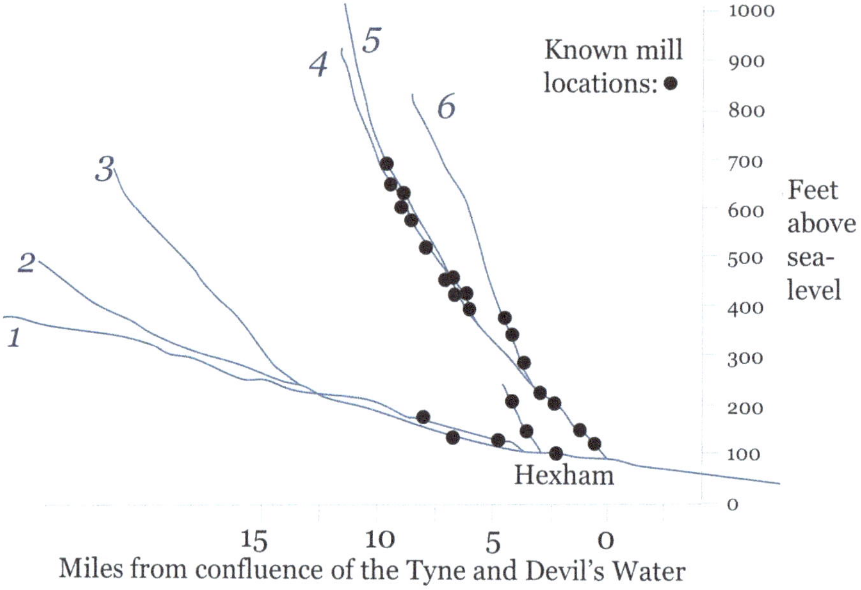

1 North Tyne **2** South Tyne **3** Allen
4 Rowley Burn **5** Devil's Water **6** West Dipton Burn.

Fig 44: Stream gradients and mill locations. This plan shows the relative steepness of the Shire's rivers compared to the Tyne valley. The vertical scale is exaggerated by a factor of 110. The location of known mills indicates the extent to which those steep gradients have been exploited to obtain water power.[2]

On the rivers upstream from Linnels the number of active mills probably more than doubled to around 14 by 1700 (see Figure 43). The greatest increase was probably in the 200 years after 1550. By the late 18th century there was more than one for each mile of river on the main streams – the Devil's Water, Dipton Burn and Rowley Burn. Many of the leats are now hard to find, but others stand out clearly, such as that in Letah Wood above Newbiggin, following the contour from the remains of a dam higher in the woods (see Figures 31 and 32 on p.43). Elsewhere, the footings of a dam can be seen quite clearly at Hallywell on the Devil's Water, where the footbridge from High Staples crosses the river. This originally raised the water level several feet to allow the leat serving Dukesfield Mill to fill, the course of which starts just across the track on the far side at the plantation edge. The leat feeding Black Hall Mill on the Rowley Burn nearby was also drawn off above a high dam, built at the usual oblique angle across the stream, now completely lost. Water supply arrangements for the Dipton Mill were quite sophisticated by 1760 (see Figure 45). The leat drawn off the burn fed, firstly the 'Whinnetly Mill', in the woods upstream from the pub, and then wound on around the hillside to a millpond immediately south of the lane that climbs to Shield Green. The pond was also supplied

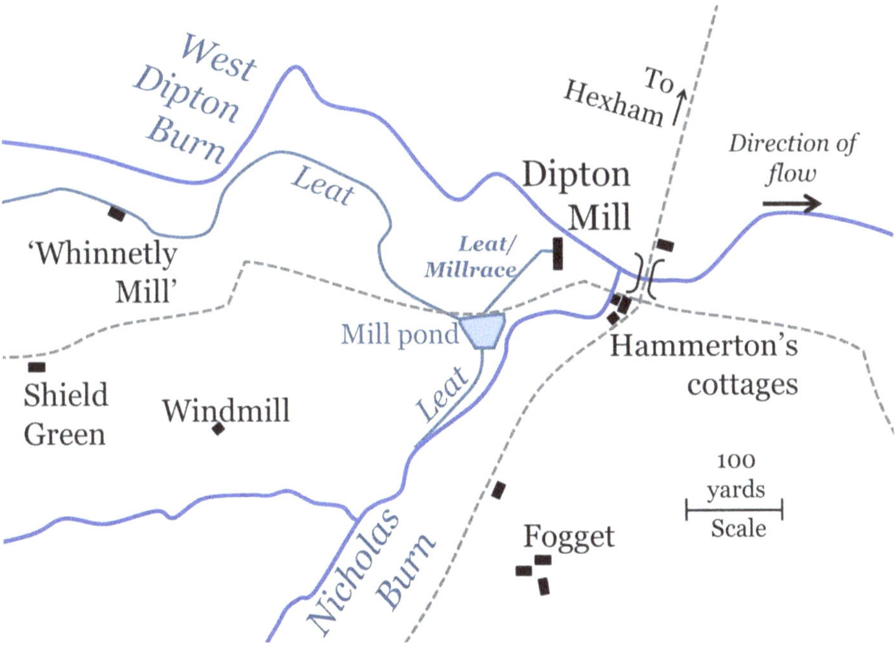

Fig 45: Dipton Mill c.1760s

by a short leat drawn off Nicholas Burn that, although usually a tiny rapid stream, drains a large area of the high ground beyond Channel Well and Loadman – as the pub has occasionally found after heavy summer rain. Sluice gates regulated the flow of water from the pond to the mill, which was roughly on the site of the stables today.[3]

What were they all for? Whitley and Newbiggin started out as corn mills, and despite the ups and downs of arable farming, so too were those built later at Black Hall, Dipton, Linnels and Dukesfield Low Mill. The majority, however, came into use for industrial purposes, several for woollen clothmaking. Some of the wool clipped from the Shire's large sheep flocks went to Hexham or more distant markets, but some was also used locally and provided an important source of employment in the 1600s and 1700s. There are several mentions of weavers in the parish registers, at Greenridge, Dotland, Whitley, Lamb Shield and elsewhere. It is safe to assume that spinning provided much additional work, for several spinners were normally needed to keep a weaver supplied with yarn.

Several of the Shire's mills were used to thicken the woven cloth to make it more waterproof by stamping the fabric in fulling or 'walk/woak' mills. A fulling mill is mentioned below Embley & Apperley in a 1569 lease, and judging from the number of fulling mills mentioned as recently built in the 1608 survey the local industry was growing in the later 16th century.

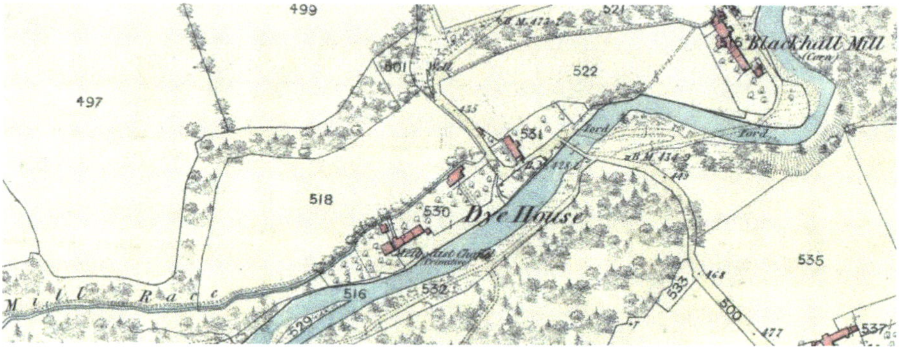

Fig 46: Mill race serving Dye House and Blackhall corn mill, downstream from Black Hall lead smelting mill (OS 6in, 1860)

One of the mills supplied by the Black Hall leat – which eventually fed the corn mill before emptying back into Rowley Burn – was used for fulling cloth in the 17th and 18th centuries. The cloth was then stretched out to dry on racks – tenters. They are shown on the 1759 Dotland enclosure map in the south-facing field above Dye House, and Tenter Hill lies behind Low Juniper. Dried cloth was also dyed and pressed here – as the name suggests – taking advantage of the soft and acidic water that was good for fixing dye. In 1747 William Angus of Juniper, fuller and dyer, bought the mill, tenters, dye house and press house, covering all the later stages of the cloth making process.[4] The mid-18th century might have marked the high point of woollen cloth making in the area, followed by gentle decline as Yorkshire's West Riding industry became increasingly competitive. But the water-powered fulling mill at Dye House and 'excellent water' were repurposed to thicken and bleach linen cloth collected from across the region in the 1780s and dried on the tenters previously used for woollens.[5]

This was not the only industry to exploit the Black Hall mill race. Up through the woods to the west, the first mill to draw its water as a power source was the Black Hall lead smelting mill, built around 1630. Lead ore, so abundant in the North Pennine hills, was converted into lead metal by being smelted at high temperature. From the 16th century this was mainly carried out in small 'ore hearths' using dried wood fuel and an air blast to achieve the required heat. The air blast was provided by large pairs of bellows driven by the mill's water power. Smelting mills typically contained a couple of hearths either side of bellows connected to the water wheel's central axle in buildings little larger than sheds. Successful operation relied heavily on the skill and experience of generally well-paid smelters. They blended ore and fuel at the right time and, crucially, at the right temperature, suffering the long-term consequences of inhaling toxic fumes to produce the 8-11 stone (50-70kg) pieces or 'pigs' of lead.

Fig 47: Burntshieldhaugh Hush, following the line of a lead vein, viewed from just to the west of the Devil's Water

While the richest lead orebodies – mineralised intrusions of ancient warm water into sedimentary rock beds – lay to the south and west around the heads of the Wear, Tees, Tyne and Allen rivers, there were a few veins in the south of the Shire. Ore could originally have been collected from the stream beds, but then dug from shallow surface pits from at least medieval times. Three good examples survive either side of the path leading down from Hackford to the Devil's Water: roughly circular mounds of upcast spoil, with a central depression. They are in a line pointing directly to Burntshieldhaugh hush opposite, the great hillside scar along the course of an SE-NW orientated lead vein (see Figure 47). Water was held back behind a dam on the moorland above, then released to strip away topsoil to reveal the ore bearing rocks below. Dating of these crude 'opencast' mines is difficult for hushing was known in the Roman period, and continued until the 19th century. The hush's depth suggests repeated use over a long period of time. Horizontal tunnels – levels, adits or soughs – were also driven into the hillsides in search of the veins. A few were tried on minor veins in the Shire, at Harwood Burn and Black Burn, possibly in the 18th century, and later the highly speculative 'Cobbler's Venture' just upstream from Crabtree Ford on the Rowley Burn in the later 19th century.[6]

The Burntshieldhaugh/Hackford lead vein seems to have been the most productive in the Shire. Joseph Blenkinsopp, a Newcastle merchant, bought Hackwood in 1744 from the Farbridge family – and for around twice its farming value.[7] Within a year Blenkinsopp was a partner in the newly formed Acton Smelt Mill eastwards across the fell. A small mill on the west bank of the Devil's Water near Hackford drove stamps that crushed the mined rock – extracted from the hush and Blenkinsopp's own shallow pits – before the fragments were sifted in water to separate ore from spoil. Hackford Mill was redundant by the 1860s. The mill buildings are shown on the OS map surveyed in 1860 but the mill race was no longer in use. Its course can be picked out by the side of the track leading down to the ford but scarcely any trace of the building remains today. Much the same applies to another old crushing mill lying right at the foot of the hush itself – just a few courses of dressed stone, still visible amongst the bracken on the Lord Crewe Estate side of the fence that divides it from Embley's land. In 1765, 320 tons of washed lead ore from here were advertised for sale by the Lord Crewe Estate.[8]

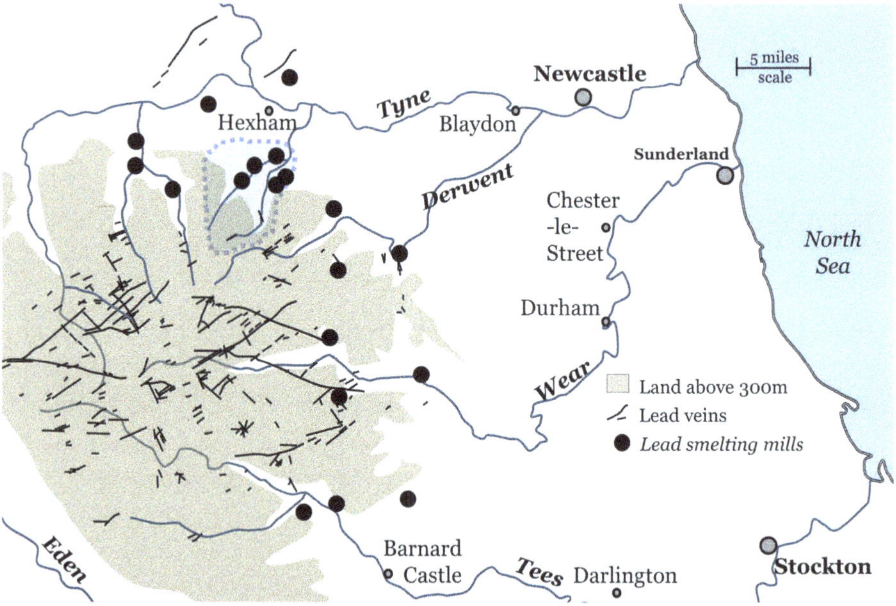

Fig 48: The North Pennines lead industry in the late 17th century. Known smelting mills lay in an arc to the north and east of the lead veins, downstream from the hills where wood fuel was available and water supply more reliable, and in the direction of the coastal ports from where the smelted lead was shipped out to London and continental Europe. The Shire lay in this arc. As peat was increasingly adopted as smelting fuel from the 1690s onwards, newer mills were located in the hills in the 18th century, such as at Nenthead. Many woodland mills were subsequently abandoned, such as at Dalton, Hathery Haugh and Red Lead Mill in Hexhamshire. Black Hall and Dukesfield continued to operate until the early 19th century.

Before the advent of ore hearth smelting using water power, lead was smelted on 'bailhills'. These were effectively glorified bonfires usually facing west to catch the prevailing wind in the hope they would achieve the required heat. An early example was found on Burntshieldhaugh Fell in the 1990s – a low grass covered mound of lead slag in charcoal rich soil, the residue of smelting.[9] Another can be seen just to the north, facing west above Gingleshaugh, given away by a scree slope of grey and sandy coloured slag upon which grass will still not grow. Others are hinted at by names left behind. Beilbrow is just west of the road south from St Helen's church, and there was a field between Juniper and Ordley named 'Bailbroom' in the late 17th century. A Dukesfield deed from 1551 mentions three bailhill sites, presumably somewhere on the hillside facing northwest.[10] Other than Burntshieldhaugh Fell these all lie to the north of the lead veins, and at first blush this seems odd. The smelters taking the Dukesfield lease in the 1550s were from Allendale, where the nearest lead mines were ten or more miles away over the fells at Sinderhope and beyond. Smelting usually reduced the weight of material by up to a half or so. Carrying ore any distance would incur the costly transport of dead weight.

This same pattern of bailhill smelting being located away from the mining zone is followed by the later mills, adopted from the early 17th century. Black Hall's was the first in the Shire in 1630, but there were four others nearby within 50 years, fairly close to each other on the Rowley Burn and Devil's Water – at Hathery Haugh, Dalton, Red Lead Mill and Dukesfield. Documentary records show that lead ore was carried to Black Hall from Hunstanworth, south of Blanchland, and from Fallowfield, beyond Acomb to the north of the Tyne, in the 1630s and later from Alston Moor. Red Lead Mill smelted lead from Teesdale, to the south, and Settlingstones, to

Fig 49: The site of Red Lead Mill. The modern track cuts through the remains of a compound above the river terrace and the remains of a mill race can be seen to the right of the track.
The mill was at work by the 1650s making red lead, used in glass making, and which required the lead ore to be smelted, refined and the resulting litharge to be reprocessed at high temperature.

the north beyond Haydon Bridge, in the 1670s. Huge quantities of lead ore were carried in to Dukesfield by galloway ponies from the Allenheads area in the 1670s. Ore came along both the aptly named Carriers' Way along the Birkside Fell ridge, and on the trackway from Sinderhope over Burntridge Moor and thence along the Lightside Road past Whitley Chapel (see Figure 42).[11] The smelting mills at Hathery Haugh (on the riverbank below and opposite the Heigh) and Dalton (the low platform of which can be seen just upstream of the road bridge over the Rowley Burn, carefully located just above the start of Whitley Mill's mill race) seem opportunistically sited close to the Lightside Road. In both cases this was perhaps to attract passing trade with claims of cheap rates during a great boom in the industry in the decades after 1660. Black Hall lead mill lies a very short distance to the north of this road, east of Whitley Chapel. In low evening sunlight, the footpath northwards past High Staples into the field beyond can be seen on a platform alongside the hedge. It then drops steeply into the woods. Today this is a rough path (see Figure 50) but signs remain that it was once a well-made track, wide enough for a cart. Access to the smelting mill must have been via a ford at the foot of this path. Dukesfield's mill had six hearths by 1675, making it almost certainly the largest lead smelting mill in Britain.[12] In those heady days, small parcels of ore carried to Dukesfield came from as far away as Dufton, overlooking the Eden Valley, and Lunehead, an extravagant 25 miles or more along the high ridges, before losing nearly half their weight when smelted.

Fig 50: 17th century trackway to Black Hall lead smelting mill northwards down to a ford across the Rowley Burn

This paradox of location is resolved when fuel – dried wood – is considered. Most mines were in uplands denuded of trees, not least as a result of medieval mining. Woodland was typically found downhill in the valleys, and it was less practical to carry bulky wood up to the mines than it was to carry sacks of compact lead ore down to the valleys. In the 18th century coal was also used as fuel. Small amounts were available from Colpitts and Kilnpit Hill southeast of Slaley, but the Stublick coal seam, not far away to the north, was worked fairly intensively in the 18th century, leaving behind the undulations of shallow pits on the moorland west of Greenridge (see Figure 8). Smelting mills also needed reliable water supplies and these were easier to find on the more mature river stretches than in the upland headwaters. Finally, the mills lay to the north east of the North Pennines mining zone, and there were others besides those in the Shire, also on the way to Newcastle, the principal regional market for lead (see Figure 48). These various benefits outweighed the cost of carrying the dead weight of ore that would be lost when smelted.

The Shire, therefore, was an attractive location for lead smelting during its great boom from the mid-17th to early 19th centuries. The mills at Hathery Haugh and Dalton do not appear to have lasted long, and Red Lead Mill was probably discontinued in the early 1700s, but smelting continued at Black Hall until the early 1800s. Dukesfield remained the largest lead mill in Britain until well into the 18th century, supplying thousands of tons of lead to Amsterdam, London, and other distant markets from the 1670s. A mile-long mill race from the dam over the Devil's Water sits on an impressive stretch of civil engineering alongside the Red Lead Mill track. The distinctive arches that mark the site today were probably added in the 1760s to carry fumes from the hearths to the stumps of chimneys on the bank, which were restored as part of the conservation and heritage project in the 2010s. In 1821 Dukesfield had 12 smelting hearths and furnaces in which silver was refined from lead. Hundreds of horses brought in ore and fuel each summer's day, and many carts were needed to carry away the lead and silver up the track that was once a well-made and graded road. The manager responsible for transport logistics from mines to mill and from mill to markets was based in Dukesfield Hall (Figure 53), and the building today should be seen as a key part of the Shire's lead industry heritage. Dukesfield Low Mill can be glimpsed across the field downstream of today's road bridge. It milled oats but even this agricultural purpose is tightly connected to the lead industry for it was built in the 1720s to provide hard feed for the many horses making their way to and from the mill from distant mines.[13]

Fig 51 (top): Stublick Chimney. A prominent early 19th century landmark on the western edge of Hexhamshire that dispersed fumes at the end of a horizontal flue which ran up the hill from Langley lead smelting mill.
Fig 52 (above): Illustrative reconstruction of Dukesfield lead smelting mill c.1800

Fig 53: Dukesfield Hall. The present farmhouse contains a great deal of 18th century work but was almost certainly originally built in the 1660s for the Blackett family's chief smelting mill and transport logistics agent John Mowbray. It was the mill agent's base until the 19th century.

This small area alongside the Devil's Water and Rowley Burn between Dye House and Dukesfield was a dense, bustling, dirty, polluting and noisy cluster of industry in the 1600s and 1700s, far removed from today's quiet pastoral landscape. Due to its regional location the Shire was a busy crossroads of long distance traffic between mines, mills and markets, and livestock on the hoof between northern pastures and London. 'Smelting Syke', set back from today's Lee Road by the width of the old wide swathe of common land was an inn on the droving route and also a resting place for horses carrying lead between Allendale and Newcastle. Perhaps this has something to do with its otherwise enigmatic name, for it was never a lead smelting mill. The overall picture is of a range of rural industry in the early modern Shire, based on the natural resources of the land, an increasingly pastoral agriculture, and its position between the uplands and the markets of Tynedale and Tyneside. Wood, wool, hides and horses were in demand as industrial raw materials and to support the transport of goods. The local economy specialised towards activities that further exploited the distinct advantages of terrain and location: the lead industry, woollen textiles, and the further development of farming in an industrial age.

[1] Hexham manor court, 30 Sept 1673: NRO 672/A/2A/131.
[2] This diagram is based on R Peel, 'Some geomorphological aspects of the Tyne drainage system' in J House (ed), *Northern Geographical Essays*, (1966), Fig 17, p.231, with new additions for other rivers in Hexhamshire and mill locations.
[3] Based on the Dotland Fell enclosure map: NRO ZGI/XXXII/4. 'Whinnetly Mill' was a cloth fulling mill, first documented in the 1608 survey (NCH III p.xx), and out of use by the time of the First edition Ordnance Survey map (1860).
[4] Hexham Manor surrenders & admittances, 12 May 1747, NRO 672/A/2A/26/2.
[5] L Sobell, 'Juniper Dye House, Bleachfield', *HH*, 30, (2020), p.29-32.
[6] R Fairbairn, *Allendale, Tynedale and Derwent Lead Mines*, (2000), p.82.
[7] Hackford & Lillswood Hall deeds 1735-1894: NRO 1888/16.
[8] Fairbairn, *op cit*, p.82.
[9] 'Lord Crewe Estate Archaeological Survey for Northumberland County Council and Lord Crewe's Charity', unpublished report by Northern Archaeological Associates, (1993).
[10] NRO B20/1. There is a 'Slaggy Hill' at 230m altitude on this hillside, though nearer Shield Hall than Dukesfield.
[11] Black Hall: NRO SANT/DEE/1/35, ZMD 147/7; Red Lead Mill: NRO 753 Box 1, Bundle J; Dukesfield: Cambridge Univ Lib MS.Add 91, Dd 7/26.
[12] G Finch, 'William Blackett, Dukesfield, and the 17th century lead industry', *HH*, 25, (2015); G Finch, *The Blacketts, A northern dynasty's rise, crisis and redemption*, (2021), pp.120, 125-7.
[13] Lead production accounts 1727-1840: NRO 672/E/1B/1-6 (available for download from Dukesfield Documents: dukesfield.org.uk/documents); 1821: Westgarth Forster, *A Treatise on a Section of the Strata, from Newcastle-Upon-Tyne, to The Mountain of Cross Fell in Cumberland*, (1821), p.416; Low Mill: NRO 672/E/1B/1.

6. Farming in an industrial age

Continued agricultural development was reflected in the level of rent commanded, roughly doubling in the course of the 17th century from two or three shillings per acre to five or more. Gair Shield provides an interesting case in point – this desolate upland shieling ground was worth 4d (old pence) per acre in 1594, no more than the going rate for 'acre money' claimed for those temporary intakes on the fell for short periods of cultivation. In 1661, however, it was let at 1s 6d/acre, over four times as much, and it doubled again to 3s 8d/acre by 1735. This degree of improvement attracted outside interest, another aspect of closer integration with the outside world. During the 17th and 18th centuries three large estates of land in the Shire took form.

In the early 17th century the Radcliffes of Dilston bought the old Ogle freehold of Aydon Shields (which the Ogles had called a manor) running up to Gair Shield, with a few outliers as at Eads Bush up at Lillswood and Whitley Mill.[1] Following the failure of the 1715 Jacobite Rising and the execution of one of its leaders, James Radcliffe, the Earl of Derwentwater, his estates were seized. They ended up in the hands of the Royal Hospital at Greenwich in 1735.

William Blackett of Newcastle bought Dukesfield in 1665 primarily as the base for the smelting mill built immediately afterwards. His son later bought land at the Steel and Dotland Park, and the lordship of the manor of Hexham from the Fenwicks of Wallington in 1689.

Ambitious copyholder John Rowland over-reached himself in buying out the other Dotland copyholders and the land fell into the determined clutches of Newcastle lawyer John Ord in 1706, who then enclosed the open arable fields.[2] His family sold to the Claverings in the 1740s, who by then also owned Embley, Low and High Eshells, the Heigh, and Harwood Shield.

Between them these three estates accounted for around half of the Shire's enclosed and improved land by the mid-18th century. They were all part of larger estates based elsewhere, so there are no grand country houses in the Shire on the scale of Dilston, Wallington (Blacketts), Axwell Park (Claverings) or Whitfield Hall (Ords). The other half of the land was owned by over three dozen other copyholders and freeholders. Their number had even increased by the early 19th century, when over half of them had less than 50 acres of land.[3] Even on the big three estates there was remarkable stability in the size of tenancies when it might have been tempting to turn the land over to large, enclosed sheepwalks watched over by a small number of shepherds. Christopher Teasdale bought all the land at Dalton but it continued in the hands of smallholding tenants. There were four tenants at Dotland before John Ord bought the land and there were still four on the enclosed land in the 1770s.

This is potentially explained by the viability of small dairy farms of 20 acres or less throughout the 18th century, supplying butter, cheese and milk to Hexham. For family farms there was probably an upper limit to the number of cows that could be milked by hand twice a day. Widow Bell of Gair Shield had just six milk kyne in the 1650s. Dorcas Ord drove dairy cattle daily between grazing ground and milking parlour at Ardley or Cook's House, and Mary Bell took butter from Nether Ardley to Hexham market in the mid-18th century. The Greenwich Hospital built lime-plastered dairies on the cooler northern sides of many of their farmhouses in the 1750s and 1760s.[4]

Eighteenth century farming therefore seems to have prospered in a Shire landscape subject to little visible change since the common fields were enclosed. Some of the steadings were improved during this period, with greater use of stone in dwellings and outbuildings. There was a further extension at Steel. Whitehall was rebuilt in 1755 and Newbiggin Hall at a similar date. However, the Greenwich Hospital and Clavering family estate accounts show continued widespread use of heather or ling thatch on steeply pitched roofs throughout the 18th century, patching up older fabric. There was a sharp decline in the population of Dotland early in the 18th century, falling from some 20 households to six or seven, but several of those who left the poorly built hamlet on a cold hilltop remained nearby elsewhere in the Shire.

While the look of the land was therefore possibly little changed over the first half of the century, the progressive enclosure of large areas of common land after 1755 had a dramatic effect. Much of the field and road layout we see today dates from five decades of planning, surveying, and building after 1750. The commons were divided amongst those with land rights. Roadways, public watering places and quarries were set out, hedged and walled. Land was cleared and new houses were built. The sequence of maps in Figure 54 shows a great wave of enclosure spreading south-westwards through the Shire.

Sir Walter Blackett, lord of the manor of Hexham, was a prime mover in the enclosure of Hexham East and West Commons in 1755 via an Act of Parliament. This was a device used increasingly through the 18th century to achieve such change where there were too many rights-holders to manage enclosure by private agreement. The subsequent division of Dotland Fell in 1759/60 was agreed privately because Blackett and the

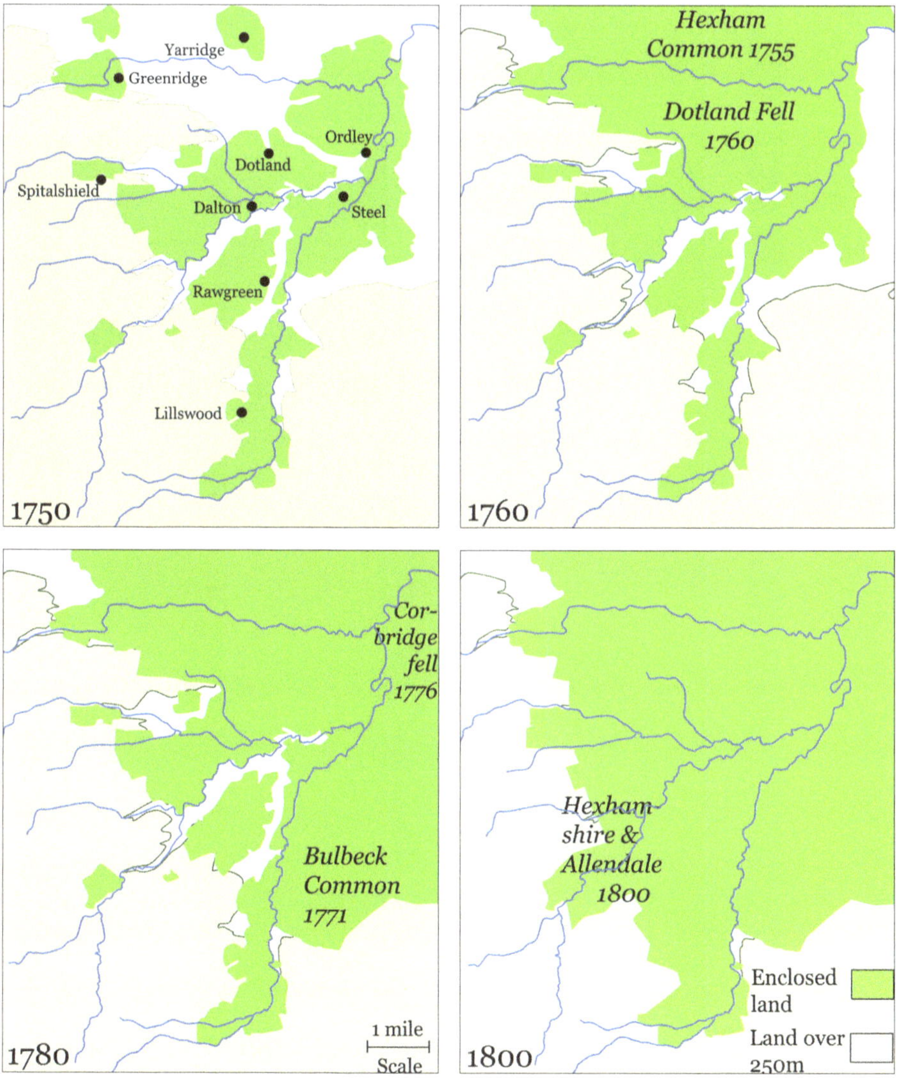

Fig 54: Successive stages of planned enclosure of common land in the second half of the 18th century, following various Acts of Parliament

Claverings easily accounted for the majority of the land concerned. Land above Dukesfield, Steel Hall, Apperley and Embley was enclosed as part of the Bulbeck Common scheme in 1771 and the now wooded heights to the east of Devil's Water above Linnel Hill were taken in from Corbridge Common in 1776. To the west, the smaller area of Nubbock and Paise Common followed in the 1780s. This left the vast Hexhamshire and Allendale commons. An ambitious proposal in 1790 to enclose the entire 45,000 acres of upland waste between the Shire and Allendale illustrates the confident spirit of improvement, in this case excessively so. It was dismissed as too ambitious

Fig 55: The geometric lines of planned enclosure boundaries and trackway viewed westwards onto the stinted common at Burntridge Moor

and a more realistic plan was introduced by the Greenwich Hospital in 1791 under which a still highly impressive 7-10,000 acres within the two parishes was eventually enclosed, a plan that took physical form on the ground from 1800.[5] It probably took 13 centuries or more before 1755 for 6-7,000 acres of land to be enclosed for cultivation and pasture. The patchy map and documentary evidence of examples of encroachment onto the fells described earlier suggests that the pace was picking up from the 17th century, but it is still likely that in the second half of the 18th century alone the enclosed area doubled as a further 8,000 acres or so were taken in from the open fell.[6]

A rising population and increased industrialisation lay behind this extraordinary burst of activity, demanding more food, raw materials and motive power for transport. The Shire's contribution remained principally of pastoral products: meat, dairy goods, wool, hides and timber. The old popular association of Midlands open field enclosure with depopulation does not apply to the great wave of upland common enclosure in the Shire. It was swiftly followed by new building (see Figure 57). Queen's Letch, Peterel Field, Black and Red Houses appeared on Hexham Common near the new straight road running down the hill. The road is in a cutting through the final bank north of the West Dipton Burn, a section that replaced the old

Fig 56: The Dipton Mill Inn was built as cottages on the land enclosed from Dotland Fell after 1760. The mill itself was located a few hundred yards to the west.

route which curved through the wood to the west to reduce the gradient. Many houses were built on Dotland Fell within a few years of its enclosure in 1760. The present Dipton Mill pub first appeared as cottages on the land granted to Richard Hammerton. The 1769 inventory of the effects of George Carr of Dotland Park showed that he had lent Hammerton the money for this. In doing so Carr was recycling agricultural profits into developing the neighbourhood, and supporting a growing population.[7] By the time of the first census in 1801 the Shire's population was more than 1,000, a rise of 25% or so in the course of the 18th century.

Another important factor was the lead industry, particularly by the time of the great enclosure of the Hexhamshire and Allendale Common. By the end of the century output from the mines and mills in the area had more than trebled since the 1750s, with most of this increase having occurred since 1780. This also trebled the demand for horse carriage, the secondary effect of which was the need for additional pasturage of reasonable quality for the fast rising population of galloway ponies. Post-enclosure tenements on the high ground such as Edge House, Lord's Lot, Low Lane House and Grouse House were ideally located to take advantage. The ruined walls of Hall Shield, possibly an ancient shieling ground, have the neat masonry

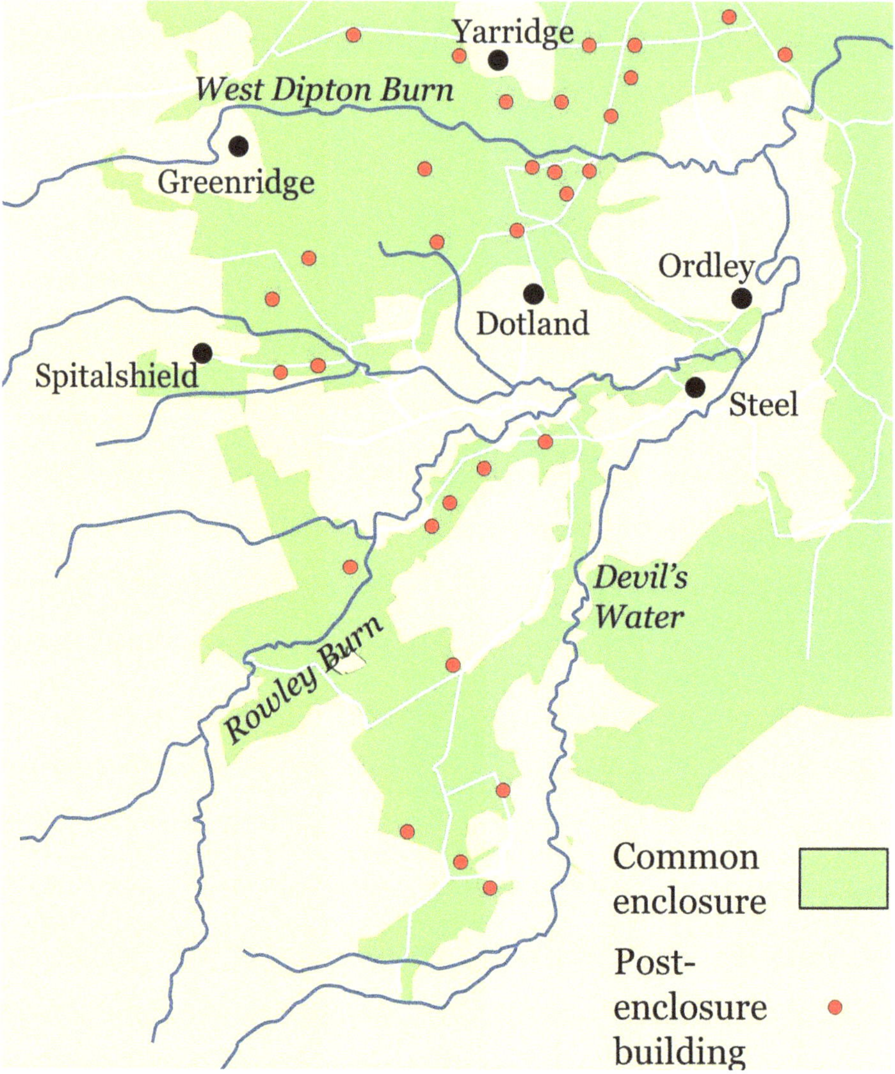

Fig 57: New building on the land enclosed from the commons, mostly in the later 18th and early 19th centuries, superimposed on the modern road network, much of which also dates from this time. Selected names of existing places and rivers given for orientation.

and wall dimensions of late 18th or early 19th century rebuilding. Many small farmers probably earned a living from carrying lead ore over the fells and grazing a dozen or so galloways in these years, such as John Hunter of Gair Shield, Joseph Rowland of Cocker Shield and Joseph Charlton of Hackford.[8] The land left unenclosed on the higher wide stretches of the Hexhamshire and Allendale Common was 'stinted' as part of the enclosure. Upland grazing was thereafter effectively rationed out in quotas – stints – proportionate to the amount of enclosed land, such was the demand.

Alongside sheep and cattle were the carrier horses; in the late 18th century common enclosures were used to meet the needs of industrial transport.

Taking in such a large amount of land from the waste took a great deal of work, hard manual work in the days before mechanised farm equipment and the internal combustion engine. Written enclosure awards set out minimum standards for roadways in some detail. North of Channel Well in 1759, for example, the drove road coming from Oxenrods was to have *'a ditch next the Road 3 ft broad and 2ft 6in deep' and the road to be level and sufficiently amended for the easy passage of Men horses carts and all manner of carriages'.* The field bank, wall, ditch, verge, level roadway, verge, hedge and bank are still clear today, the boundaries 12 yards (11m) apart as specified in 1759 (see Figure 58).[9] A few hundred yards westwards from where it crosses the main road, itself set out in the 1759 enclosure award, the old drove road turns sharply to the right on its way to Oxenrods and on the corner a watering place was set aside for the driven livestock. Behind it can still be seen the sandstone face of the public quarry. Based on the amount of land taken in, the lengths of distinctive wide, straight roads and the approximate average size of new, square fields, around 220 to 230 miles of hedge, ditch and wall were planted, dug and built from the 1750s onwards. Many of the circular sheepfolds and stells can still be seen dotted around the remaining stinted fell land above the new enclosures.

Fig 58: Post-enclosure walling, ditching and levelling of the Oxen Road looking westwards near Channel Well, following the details set out in the 1759 Enclosure Award

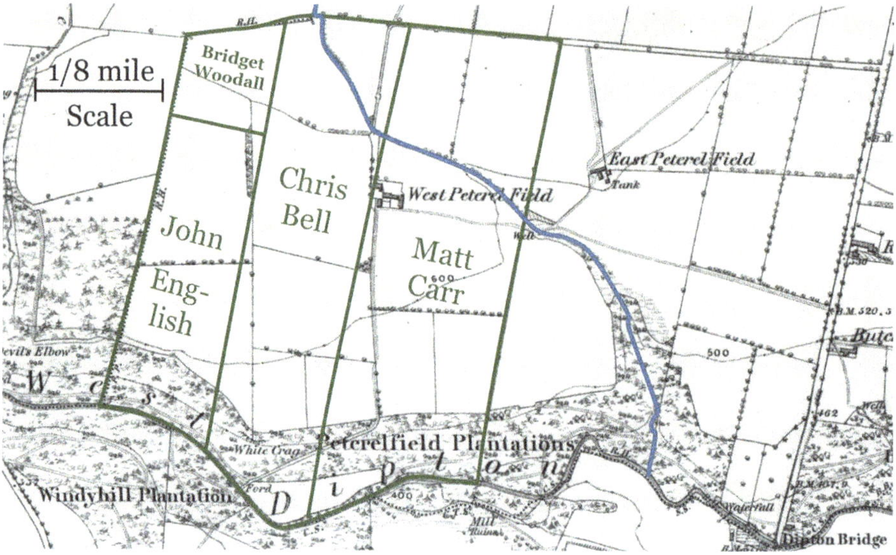

Fig 59: An example of varying field arrangement following the 1755 enclosure of Hexham Common. The allotments awarded in the West Peterel Field area, and their boundaries, are overlain on the OS 6in map surveyed in 1860. By 1802 the four original allotments were all in the hands of Christopher Bell, and the later field boundaries differ from those of the original award. By contrast, around East Peterel Field the boundaries still follow those set out in the 1755 award.

The cost of this 'infrastructure work' would have been beyond the means of many of those granted common allotments. On Hexham Common, enclosed in the 1750s, the number of landowners fell from 117 to 47 between 1752 and 1805.[10] A small example of this consolidation can be seen in Figure 59, where Christopher Bell, a Greenwich Hospital agent and lessee of a colliery at Stublick in the 1760s and 1770s, was awarded 31 acres in 1755. By 1802 he was also the owner of adjacent land and had aligned his fields to a different pattern.

Those boundaries, as elsewhere on the old Hexham East Common, are mainly hedged, albeit usually set on a few courses of stonework. So too is much of the Dotland Fell land. Hedges of hawthorn, gorse and holly flank the drove road, today's bridleway, once it clears the Dipton Burn woods northwards and climbs up the old Hexham East Common immediately west of the racecourse. The hedge was intended to be prickly enough to deter the escape of livestock. A careful look at the walled enclosures higher up the Shire shows that much of the new land there too was originally hedged. Across the valleys in June the hawthorn in blossom appears as broken white lines against the bright green fields. They are broken because many of these hedges failed. Often today lone hawthorns are the sole remains of a grown-out hedge alongside the stone wall that replaced it. It might have been difficult to find enough seedlings to start the huge distances of 'quick hedge' required in the first place, but even when they were available it would have been even harder to protect the new hedges from enthusiastic grazing stock in the years before barbed wire. Hazel hurdles were the preferred protectors but hazel was highly sought-after by the rapidly expanding regional coal industry for corves or baskets. Contemporary writers bemoaned the state of the hedges. A Scottish visitor in 1814 commented that in Northumberland *'the ragged Hedges make a bad fence, and composed of Hawthorn, Honeysuckle, Crabs, Hazel &c formed a strong contrast to the well-dressed hedges we had left in the north'.*[11]

As if the fencing or walling of the new lands was not enough, many of the existing fields on Greenwich Hospital land were also reconfigured soon afterwards, as shown and described in Figure 60, a sequence of maps around Aydon Shields and Salmonfield. Elsewhere, an 1802 map of the Hospital's estate at Wooley, to the east of Devil's Water, is annotated with the plan for grubbing up the ancient boundary lines and replacing them with more regimented successors. The Hospital had the capital available for this work across its 800 acres of land in Hexhamshire, whether undertaken directly or by making rent allowances to its tenants to the same end. On smaller owner-occupied farms such as Litharge, where William Martin had 31 acres, Whitehall (Thomas Johnson senior and junior, 90 acres) and Hackford (Anthony Leaten, 34 acres) there is little sign of changing field alignments between 1792 and 1860, nor of much encroachment into the common before the 1800 Enclosure Act. However, intermediate landowners such as Edward Charlton (280 acres in 1800) and William Ord (155 acres) had been taking in land from the common around their farms at Low and High Ardley, Walley Thorn and Cook's House according to the 1792 pre-enclosure plans. The old bulbous form of the medieval boundaries was already by then starting to be erased by neater field boundaries and no trace can be seen by the time of the 1860 Ordnance Survey.

The work was worth it because regularly shaped fields were easier to plough. More grain was needed to meet the demand for food from Britain's fast growing population following the outbreak of the wars with France in 1793 and consequent disruption to imports. Some of the increased grain production came from increasing the frequency of sowing for crops within existing rotation cycles, and some by ploughing up some of the higher land, probably for the first time in a widespread fashion since the medieval peak 500 years before. Traces of this wartime high tide of arable farming in the hills can be seen in rig and furrow patterns that are straighter and

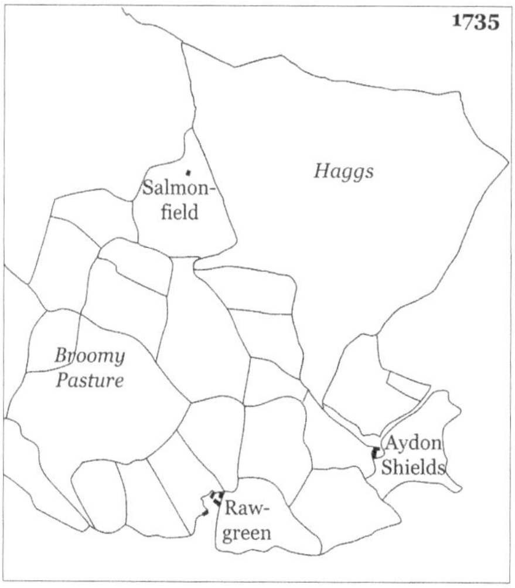

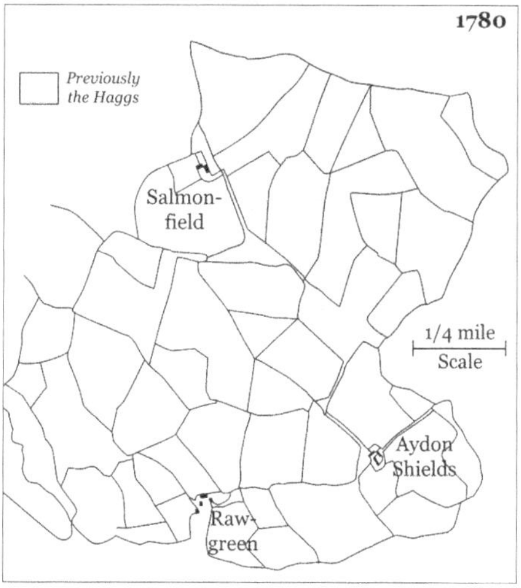

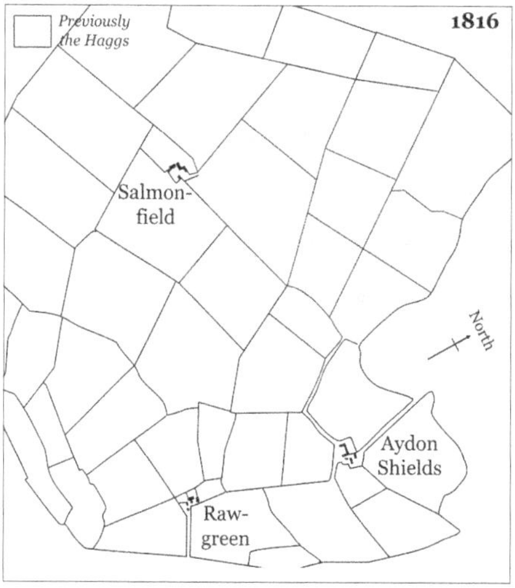

Fig 60: This succession of maps, based on estate plans drawn up for the Greenwich Hospital, brings out the extent of change in 18th century field layout in the Aydon Shields area. In 1735 the 'Haggs' (in particular) and 'Broomy Pasture' were old and large enclosures, their names indicating poor quality land used as rough pasture. Both had been divided into smaller and irregular enclosures by 1780. By 1816, however, the land had been reorganised into much more regular fields, better suited to arable farming during wartime. Only the sinuous boundary to the north west was unaltered. It marked the property division between Aydon Shields and High Holms, as it still does today, and possibly has done since the likely creation of the Aydon Shields estate in the early medieval period.

Maps derived from: 1735: TNA MPII/1/40/3; 1780 & 1816: Allendale Estate collection.

narrower than the wide medieval reversed S curves. Lighter ploughs were in use, increasingly drawn by horses rather than long teams of oxen. An extensive example can be seen on LiDaR (Figure 61) within the enclosure allotment to the west of High and Low Eshells at 980ft altitude (300m).

Given the increased grain production of the war years it was awkward that the Dipton Mill had burnt down a few years earlier, in 1783. There is actually no sign that it was ever put back into production, for mill races or ponds are not shown on an 1820 estate map.[12] Other corn mills in the area must have responded instead to the wartime increase in grain production. Linnels mill was rebuilt and its oat-roasting kiln installed in around 1800,[13] and it's reasonably likely that the windmill up on the hill

Fig 61: The regular lines of early 19th century wartime ploughing within the enclosure allotment west of Eshells, visible in LiDaR imagery. They contrast with the less regular pattern of older temporary intakes slightly to the north, which do not respect the enclosure boundaries. The wider edged features to the lower left mark out firebreaks between more recent patches of heather-burning.

south of the Dipton burn, now the Thruff, dates from around the same time.

The high wartime price of food was desperate for the labouring poor, but coming after a good 150 years of agricultural prosperity this great wartime farming boom must have made farming seem even more of a 'one way bet' to those with land. Rents had increased steadily during the 1700s. Gair Shield's 3s 9d/acre in 1735 was increased to 5s 6d when it was next let in 1758, and nearly 6s in 1789. The Staples, better ground, was let for 10s/acre in 1758, but 13s/acre 30 years later. Rental income from the Greenwich Hospital's estate increased threefold between the 1730s and 1790s. Rents then soared when tenancies fell in during wartime. A Greenwich Hospital survey of 1805 set out a plan to be followed when the farm leases expired in 1809:

> *'it is occupied at present by a set of industrious tenants, but not of a description we fear to make much improvement, nor is the property of a nature likely to invite the attention of farmers of large capital and enterprising spirit; some improvements have however been made by the present occupiers, and a considerable advance of rent may be expected at the next letting, when it is hoped that farmers of a better description will come forward.'* [14]

These social engineering aspirations were not entirely carried through, but some new names do appear on the leases after 1809 – Robert Coulson at Salmonfield, possibly moving in from Lanchester, and the Thorburns at Rowley Head, replacing the long standing Nevin family tenants. Mary Nevin had paid 7s 8d/acre; Andrew and John Thorburn signed up at 17s. Aydon Shields had commanded just over 8s/acre in 1789 but was let at over 20s in 1809. Similar increases were obtained elsewhere in the Shire. Farmhouses and outbuildings were rebuilt as part of the attraction. In 1817 the Greenwich Hospital's surveyor reported that

> *'the Farm-Houses have been enlarged by being made what is termed square, thereby affording additional Lodging Room for the Families of the Tenant; the enlargement of the Farms occasioned by the division of uncultivated Lands, or the consolidation of smaller establishments, having produced a more respectable and enterprising tenantry than could be expected on farms of lesser magnitude.'* [15]

Once again, the Greenwich Hospital led the way, building the solid foursquare steadings that we see today. The old houses and cottages are often still there, used as outbuildings. Raw Green was rebuilt in 1810, so too Gair Shield, and the old house converted into a stable. Since other estates were also competing for those 'more respectable and enterprising tenantry'

Fig 62: Salmonfield. The Greenwich Hospital farmhouse of 1813 is at right of centre, with older accommodation to its left and right, and 19th century outbuildings around the yard. The west-facing 1920s 'County Farm' can be seen at top left.

Fig 63: Early 19th century country respectability – William Ord's High Holms

they had to follow suit. The Claverings, doubtless aware of the Hospital's intentions, rebuilt Dotland and Embley to the same square plan in 1807 when their leases fell in (see Figures 64 and 65).[16] An 1812 penny found under a staircase at Ordley when it was restructured in modern times suggests major improvements there at around the same time. Extensions to Stobby Lea and High Holms (see Figure 63) have the look of the same period, in all probability built by William Ord, at that time also owner of Ardley and Walley Thorn. High Holms' old bastle was by then an outbuilding and newer ones were added during these war years. More highly capitalised farms needed outbuildings for additional workhorses, livestock and machinery for threshing the extra corn. Threshing machinery was driven by horse-power in adjacent circular sheds, 'gin-gangs', some of which survive as at High Staples, Ardley and Black Hall (Figure 67).

The great changes of the French revolutionary and Napoleonic war period have left a distinctive mark on today's landscape, from the solid, foursquare farmsteads to the regular field edges and the enclosed commons with their straight and wide roadways. It can often be hazardous to ascribe the origin of economic and social changes to specific events or short periods but it's equally hard to escape the impression that the 22 years of the French wars really did have a big impact on the farming economy, the look

Fig 64 (top): Dotland, and *Fig. 65:* Embley, c.1920. Substantial farmhouses built by the Clavering family in 1807, almost certainly to compete with the Greenwich Hospital for enterprising tenants during the farming boom of the Napoleonic War years

of the land, and to widen the gap between the landed and the landless. As farms became larger, costlier and tenanted by more 'respectable' famers, cottage accommodation was often provided next to the steading, such as at Turf House, Salmonfield and at High Staples. It meant – as the Greenwich

Hospital's surveyor put it in 1817 – *'that the tenant is enabled constantly to overlook and control his Labourers'.*

However, at the end of the war in 1815, the market went into reverse. A great farming depression followed which lasted for more than twenty years. It must have been a devastating shock to landowners and tenants after such a long farming boom, a rude awakening from the dream of the 'one way bet', and brought desperation for many newly unemployed labourers. After at least a century and a half of rises, rents started falling. At Peacock House in 1817 *'This rent has lately been reduced from £95 to £72 in consequence of the tenant being permitted to relinquish his lease from the depression of the times.'* Many farms were consolidated into larger concerns in these years. The four separate holdings at Dotland that had survived through the 18th century became two by 1808, and were then combined into the one vast farm of 840 acres in 1820. The Greenwich Hospital's land at Heckley House, up on the ridge between Rowley Head and Salmonfield, was divided between those adjacent farms in 1809 and the steading at Heckley disappeared from the map. Dalton's five separate small tenancies were still there in 1799 but had been combined into a single large farm of 250 acres before 1830. Those small and ancient holdings at the Steel, mapped in 1802, were shown on the 1839 tithe map as a single farm.

Depression also exposed limits to improvements in the wake of the extensive Hexhamshire and Allendale common enclosure of 1800. The maps and reports of the Greenwich Hospital certainly show a great deal of change on its land within just a few years during the war years, but even with the resources of this great estate progress was slow. It is likely that change was slower still on the allotments granted to people of limited means. The Hospital estate survey of 1805 found that very little of their common 'allotment' land had been improved by then, five years after the enclosure award, but by 1817 the land had been mostly broken in around Gair Shield, Rowley Head and Salmonfield. On the other hand, a bleak picture of Rawgreen and Turf House was drawn by the Hospital's agent, John Grey in 1835, after 20 years of farming depression.

> *'These are the two farms to which that description of Moor Land would be the most useful & to which also it is the nearest. The interior fences consisting of stone walls, are entirely in ruins & to rebuild them, would be to imitate the folly that first projected the division of such miserable land into Fields of fifteen acres as if it would have grown wheat and Turnips'.*[17]

Fig 66: An early 19th century labourer's cottage next to the Greenwich Hospital's High Staples farm. *'The tenant is enabled constantly to overlook and control his Labourers'.*

Fig 67: Gin-gang at Black Hall, a circular horse-walk providing power to drive machinery for the adjacent threshing barn, probably dating to the early 19th century.

It is hardly surprising that the Shire's population reached a peak of 1,130 people in 1831 that it has not regained since. Many people moved away to the growing towns and cities. Edward Stobbs, whose family had long been established on the small holding at Hathery Haugh, right next to the Rowley Burn, moved to North Shields; and Samuel Johnson from Whitehall was across the estuary at South Shields. Some of the new building on Dotland Fell after the 1760 enclosure was gone by the middle of the 19th century: Nicholas Hall was empty by the time of the 1841 census, Oxenrods by 1851. Hall Shield was abandoned to its current fate after 1841.

The population fall would probably have been more dramatic had it not been for the persistence of the lead industry. Gair Shield's tenant in 1817, John Hunter, was a lead ore carrier, and could evidently still pay the rent set in 1809 through grazing his galloway ponies on the unforgiving

Fig 68 (top): Hall Shield, west of Edge House, and *Fig 69:* Winter House, on the north flank of the Rowley Burn. Small farm steadings abandoned in the 19th century

Fig 70: Hexhamshire population in the 19th century (High, Middle and Low Quarters)

land. The continued need for carriage ponies possibly explains the further subdivision of the common allotments documented in an 1839 survey.[18] However, when Dukesfield Mill closed in 1835 it dealt a terminal blow to ore and lead carriage by the Shire's tenant farmers. This had a severe impact on the viability of their small pasture holdings, contributing to the bleak outlook described by John Grey at Rawgreen and Turf House on his tour of the estate that year.

At the Steel the smallholdings might have been consolidated into a single farm, but the hamlet remained because of the eight households recorded there in the 1851 census. Two were occupied by farm labourers and six by lead smelters. Theirs was a skilled enough trade that even 16 years after the closure of the nearby smelt mill at Dukesfield they continued to be employed at their Beaumont landlord's larger Allen Mill below at Catton, walking to their week-long shifts over the moors past Eshells and back. The survival of the Steel as a hamlet is a subtle legacy of the lead industry for it was otherwise likely to have been swept away during the lean years of the early 19th century.

Farming fortunes improved again in the third quarter of the century, leading to a further wave of investment in farms, farmyards and also the fields by the larger estates. The remains of Dotland village were swept away in 1854, and solid Victorian outbuildings put up behind the farmhouse. Byres and two-storey haysheds were arranged in the large regular Northumbrian

Fig 71: Detail of field drains marked on a mid-19th century plan of Dotland Park, owned by the Beaumonts (successors to the Blacketts), the drain pipes for which probably came from the Dukesfield Tile Works. One such drain on adjacent Dotland farmland to the south empties into a roadside ditch on the Lee Road, the road seen here crossing the bottom left of the map.

pattern around a square yard. Covered barns suitable for collecting cattle manure helped sustain the fertility of land used for arable cropping and stock fattening in the mid-19th century. The adjacent labourer's cottage at Dotland was literally and figuratively below the farmhouse (see Figure 89). Other small square farmyards also appeared in the Victorian period, such as at Dalton and Low Ardley. On higher ground to the south, the fertility of the area's naturally acidic soil was enhanced by applying lime, burned in stone kilns, one of which survives next to the Linn Burn just below Westburnhope.

This was also the great age of field drainage, huge outlays being made to improve the heavy clay land to make it easier to work. Many are the field plans of the large estates with their parallel lines of clay pipes. On these estates the agents were powerful and influential instruments of change. John Grey, who moved from North Northumberland to Dilston in the mid-1830s to become the Receiver of the Northern Estates of the Greenwich Hospital, arguably had a greater impact on local farming than any other individual during the Victorian period. He was a respected

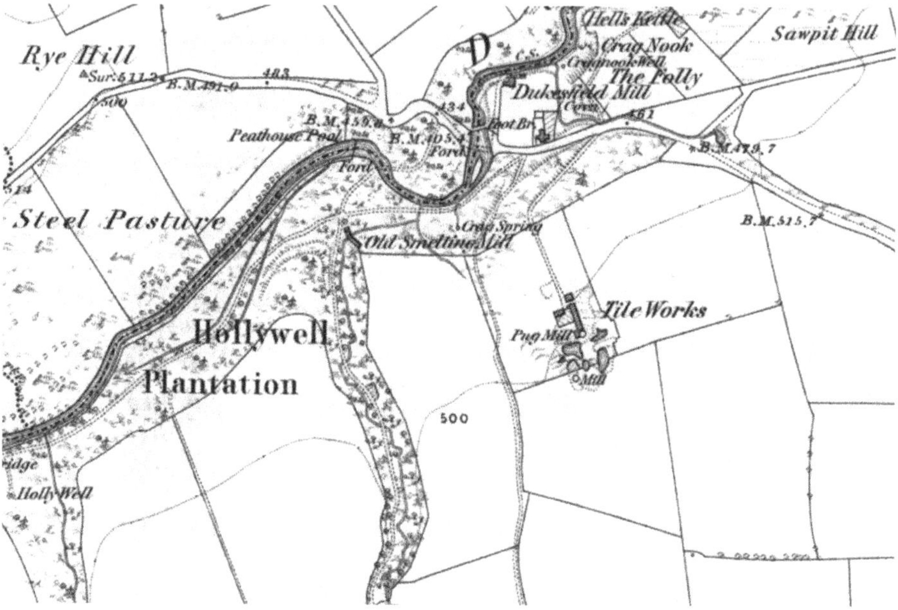

Fig 72: Dukesfield Tile Works in 1860, catering to local demand in the heyday of Victorian field drainage

member of the Royal Agricultural Society, had papers published in its annual journal, and saw field drainage as the main source of a rental improvement of 25% during the 1850s, justifying the initial capital cost of material, carriage and labour. Dilston Hall was built for Grey. Land agents also helped agriculture to drive industrial activity. The Blackett estate, by now in the hands of the Beaumont family, built a brick and tile works in the field above the old Dukesfield smelt mill at around this time. Complete with a puddle mill, firing kiln and drying sheds, the production of 2 inch field drain pipes was one of its main outputs, supplied to farms on the Beaumont estate (see Figure 72).

A flurry of chapel building, paid for by the subscriptions of local nonconformist churchgoers, illustrates the optimism of the high Victorian period. Over 30 such chapels were put up between 1840 and 1875 across the North Pennines.[19] In the Shire, Dye House's Primitive Methodist chapel was opened in 1865. Lillswood and Whitehall Methodist chapels were both opened in 1871 little more than a mile apart, and subscriptions also paid for a school at Lillswood in 1830. Whitley Chapel's school was rebuilt in 1849 and Ordley's was open before the 1890s. Dalton's small corrugated iron chapel was dismantled in 1965, but the others, including the Methodist chapel at Finechambers at the top of Juniper village, are still there today, all now put to other uses.

19th century non-conformist chapels.
Fig 73 (top left): Dye House (1865)

Fig 74 (above): Lillswood and
Fig 75 (left): Whitehall, both opened in 1871, scarcely more than a mile apart

The opening of Whitehall and Lillswood chapels in 1871 marked the high point of Victorian confidence, for they came just before the onset of what was traditionally seen as the long 'great depression' of English farming from the mid-1870s through to the 20th century. A reduction in cropping meant there was much less traffic to the local corn mills. Finechambers and Linnels both gave up the trade during the 1880s. In October 1873 William Johnson, the owner of Whitley Mill, thought that 'it will be the best way to lay no more money out in repairs but to let her go down and to dispose of the machinery for what it will bring'. A wearied concern over the state of farming runs throughout Johnson's correspondence.[20] There was little money available for further building improvements. In response to a request from the tenants at Hamburn Hall a few years later, he retorted that *'I think Lowdon & his family had better live in the warm kitchen in the winter, as others have done, than put me to the expense of building a porch at the back door.'*

This co-incided with the collapse of the lead price in the 1880s, which saw off the remnants of mining in the Shire. Population continued to fall, reducing by over a quarter in the last 30 years of the century. Pubs closed – the Sportsman at Lillswood, the Three Tuns at Dalton and the old droving stop at Smelting Syke. Marginal tenements such as Winter House and Hathery Haugh on either side of the Rowley Burn below the Lightside

Road were abandoned in the 1880s and 1890s, their quiet ruined walls still decaying well over a century later.

The 'great depression' in farming is, however, too sweeping a generalisation. It had far more impact in the arable lands of the south and east of England. Pastoral farming fared better. Adaptation might mean survival. 28% of Dotland's 850 acres grew grain crops in 1853. In 1912 it was just 8%, illustrating the further shift to meat and dairy farming.[21] Sheep, cattle and liquid milk for the urban markets on Tyneside could be moved by rail from Hexham. This possibly sustained frugal livelihoods on small farms without the need for extensive outbuilding redevelopment on the Victorian courtyard pattern seen elsewhere on the larger mixed farms. Turf House retained its byre in line with the dwelling house. When Hesleywell was sold as a 48 acre farm in 1924 its old bastle opposite the farmhouse served as byre for 20 cattle with lofts above. A hay house, pig stye and cart shed made up the rest of the outbuildings.[22] In the interest of economy, where new buildings were needed they tended to be made of cheap materials, such as with the introduction of corrugated iron towards the end of the 19th century. An example can still be seen at Stublick Hill, to the left of the road from Hexham to Allendale.

A branch of the Stobbs family came back from the coast and took on Dalton. Whitley Mill's owner, Reverend James Johnson, decided not to demolish it after all and, in the face of a brief upturn in trade in 1879, agreed to repair the mill and its wheel. It survived as a mill until the 1920s. Corn was no longer ground at Linnels but the mill's water power was used instead to generate electricity, providing the first such lighting in the Shire.[23] The larger estates continued investing through the lean years, and farms at Salmonfield and Low Staples, for instance, had domestic extensions built in the Edwardian years. Another significant investment in the 1870s and 1880s came to have a marked impact on the Shire's landscape – the creation of the 600 acre Fell Plantation on the poor high ground above Dukesfield by the Beaumonts.

Forestry

Forestry plantations were long-term investments but worthwhile for the eventual value of harvested timber, especially when alternative uses of the land offered little prospect of decent returns. Woodland had, of course, always been important. Until the late 18th century it had mainly comprised native broadleaved hardwoods in the hedges, along the riverbanks and in small enclosures, the worked remnants of ancient natural land cover. Coppicing was widely practised, cutting new growth every decade or so

Fig 76: Post-enclosure forestry plantations on Greenwich Hospital land providing wind breaks to Gair Shield (centre right) and to the north on Burntridge.

to provide mine props, coal basket (or corfe) rods, and lead smelting fuel. Fairly small areas of woodland, worked in rotation, could therefore provide a constant supply of material. Old coppiced trees, now grown out in the century or so since the practise stopped, can still be seen widely, such as alongside the footpaths through West Dipton Burn (see Figure 79) or in Letah Woods. Larger trees were periodically felled for construction and carpentry timber. Their valuable tannin-rich oak bark was then stripped off and used in leather tanning.

Hexham's growing leather industry, itself based originally on the area's livestock farming, was just part of a widespread national increase in the demand for bark that saw the price quadruple in just 30 years after 1780.[24] This gave strong encouragement to the planting of new woodland. Over 500 acres of Corbridge Common, on the eastern heights above Devil's Water, were planted with mostly broadleaved trees during these years. Today, the West Dipton Burn woods near the old drove road crossing feel quite natural but the well-spaced and very tall mature oak and beech trees show they were planted on purpose and managed actively, in this case

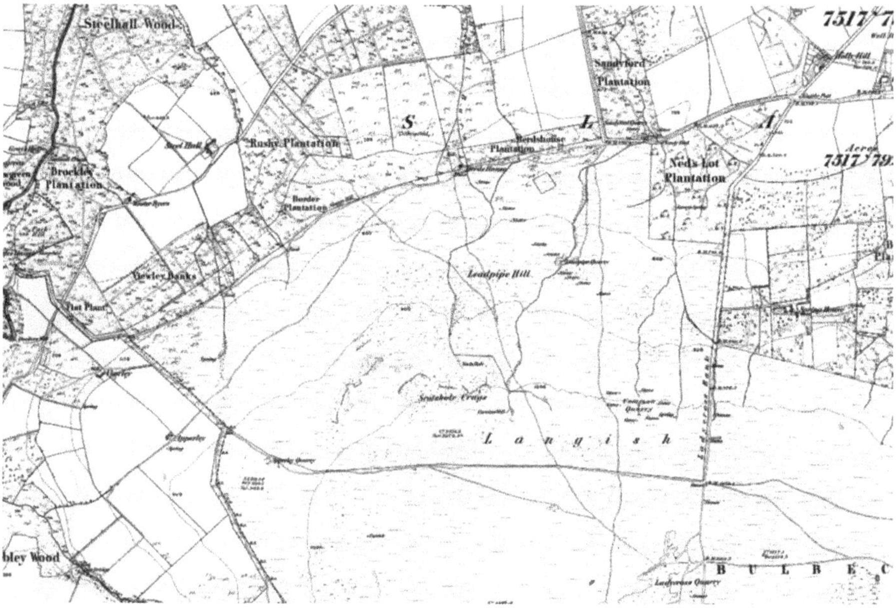

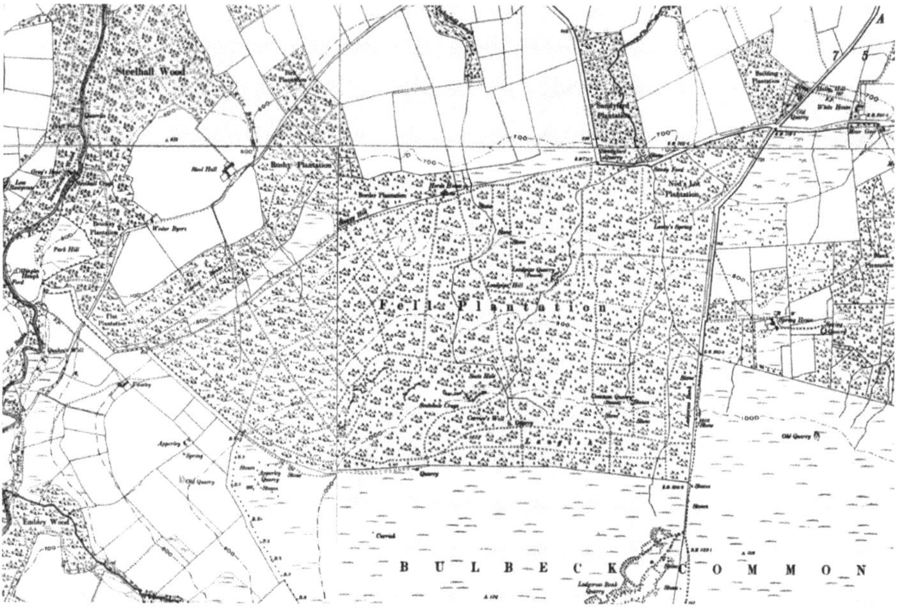

Figs 77 and 78: Fell Plantation south of Dukesfield in 1860 (top) and 1895

following the enclosure of Hexham common in the 1750s. However, slow-growing oak trees could not keep pace with demand for bark so the first major inroads of fast-growing conifers were planted towards the end of the 18th century, principally larch. Its bark, though greatly inferior to oak for leather tanning, did at least produce some tannin, unlike other conifers.

Fig 79: Old coppice beech in the Dipton woods. The footpath alongside the West Dipton Burn runs through plantations of beech and oak established after the Hexham Common enclosure of 1755

Some of the present large conifer plantations in the area were originally planted with oak, such as Steelhall Wood and Dipton Wood on Corbridge Fell.

Shelter belt plantations of larch and Scots fir pine were planted by the Greenwich Hospital to the west of Gair Shield and on Burnt Ridge after the 1800 common enclosure to give some protection from the prevailing wind, meet demand for bark, and provide timber to an organisation conditioned by its naval connections to value the commodity highly. The Board of Agriculture's surveyors of Northumberland in 1805 remarked that *'plantations on an extensive scale are rising in every part of the county, and are almost in every instance doing well ... the larch rises proudly pre-eminent above the rest'.*[25] Scots fir and Norwegian spruce became more popular as the price of bark fell back again after 1810, making larch less attractive.

Towards the end of the 19th century the Fell Plantation above Dukesfield added to the large areas of managed woodland on the higher ground (see Figures 77 and 78). Farming employment declined in these decades, but as many woodsmen were enumerated in the 1891 census in the Shire as in 1871. Slaley Forest, to the east of Fell Plantation, and significantly larger at nearly 2,000 acres in size, was mostly planted in the

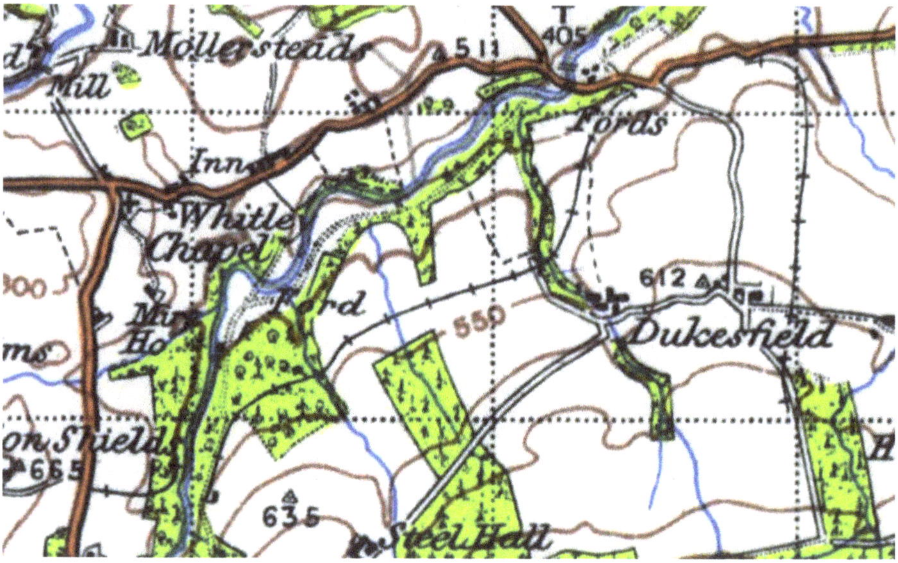

Fig 80: Light forestry railways in 1921

1930s after the land was acquired by the Forestry Commission. This state body was created in the 1920s to give impetus to forestry following the timber shortages experienced during World War One.[26]

Timber harvesting was responsible for an interesting and short lived feature of the local landscape. The 1921 OS map shows the course of three light railways (see Figure 80). One ran for a short distance from the woods west of the Devil's Water to the road near Aydon Shields and another was laid from Steelhall Wood for more than a mile around the contours to the Dukesfield road end. It was worked by a small steam engine for bridges on trellises across the burns meant the use of horsepower was impractical. Another line dropped northwards downhill from Sandyford Plantation past Middle Dukesfield to the bridge at Heron's Burn. It lay next to a First World War German POW camp, which provided the labour to build these tracks, and the bridge over the Heron's Burn. The lane junction where the Dukesfield track ended was sometimes called 'The Ziplins', perhaps a lingering reference to German wartime labour – Zeppelins. Timber could be led away by traction engine from here towards the Traveller's Rest and onwards to Tynedale without having to negotiate the difficult fords through the Shire. Gravity enabled empty trucks at the Heron's Burn bridge to be brought back up the slope by the descent of the loaded ones.[27] The trackbed of the Aydon Shield railway can just about be seen from the footpath in from Low Rawgreen northeastwards to the Devil's Water. Taking the permissive footpath from Dukesfield Arches towards the farm, the level trackbed of the Steelhall Wood line can still be seen – faintly – in the field to the west as the path rises clears of woodland. Once the timber was hauled away the rails proved useful elsewhere. At least one still supports the now quite precarious bridge over the Hall Burn on the permissive path.

When the forests were harvested there was work for sawmills. Reprieved by Rev Johnson in the 1870s, Whitley Mill, the first mill built in the Shire, was also the last to close, finishing its days as a sawmill between 1918 and 1935. Mature timber felled in the plantations originally established by the Greenwich Hospital in Hexhamshire was sawn and creosoted (for weather protection) at Rushwood to provide local building and fencing supplies in the 1920s. Temporary sawmills also operated at Stotsfold Hall during the Second World War, and another was at work near the old Dukesfield smelt mill's arches in the 1970s.[28]

Country retreats

Another response by the large estates to the late Victorian farming depression was the steady increase in grouse shooting that – like forestry – remains as an actively managed element of today's landscape. Springtime swaling or burning of the heather encourages the growth of succulent new shoots, favoured as food by the red grouse, and has given rise to the moorland patchwork on the high ground, amidst the isolated shooting huts

Fig 81: Stotsfold Hall – a summer residence for the Sunderland Mounsey family

and trackways. The 'Drag Road' which branched from the Lightside Road alongside the Rowley Burn and climbed over the heights to Allendale gave easier access for the Beaumonts to their shooting grounds. Grand country retreats were constructed. The dramatic neo-gothic Duke's House mansion on the ridge looking southwards over the Devil's Water was built for Edward Backhouse, a Darlington banker, in 1873. Stotsfold Hall (Figure 81) was built as a summer residence by Backhouse relatives in the Mounsey family, Sunderland shipbuilders, in 1901-2. Linnels House was built in the 1890s for the Charltons of Cullercoats. The same decade saw the establishment of Hexham Racecourse on the Yarridge estate by Charles Henderson, another incoming industrialist from County Durham. Its facilities were extended in the 20th century. The course probably replaced a more informal horseracing course that had been located somewhere on the common nearby in the 1670s, when it was mentioned as the destination of a trackway near the West Dipton burn.[29] Victorian shooting boxes, country retreats and a racecourse faintly echo the construction of Dotland Park as a medieval retreat by Hexham Priory, but with the fruits of industrial enterprise rather than from landed monastic wealth.

Fig 82: Hexham racecourse on the gentle south-facing slope at Yarridge above the West Dipton Burn, viewed from the east. The old drove road, now a bridleway, crosses from centre left to right immediately beyond the course.

[1] G Finch, 'Under the unlawful defence of some mighty person. The disputed estate of Aydon Shields in late Tudor Hexhamshire', *HH*, 21 (2011).
[2] Finch, 'Dotland deserted?', *op cit.*
[3] Compiled from the Hexhamshire and Allendale Common Enclosure award 1800: NRO 691/62/8, and High and Middle Quarters Tithe awards and plans of 1839: NRO DT /243, 245.
[4] L Sobell, 'Holmes, Sweet Holmes', *HH* 11, (2001); Greenwich Hospital Northern estate accounts: TNA ADM 68/303.
[5] L Sobell, 'Beating about the bush about the boundaries; the struggle to enclose Hexhamshire and Allendale Commons, *HH* 24, (2014); John Bell to J E Blackett, 10 Mar 1793, NRO 11603. Prior to measurement the area was initially thought to comprise an even more ambitious 60,000 acres. The remaining common land was 'stinted' to manage the amount of stock to be grazed.
[6] Earlier encroachments, whether permitted at the time they were made or not, were invariably formally recognised under the various enclosure awards. Their extent was measured to ensure they were excluded from the acreage of 'antient inclosures' used to determine awards of allotments from the common, but where those pre-enclosure encroachments can be compared with later maps, such as at the Eshells, the earlier boundaries of encroachments survived – and in the same hands.
[7] Johnson of Dotland Park papers, NRO 3543.
[8] Ore carrier payments, Dukesfield 1814: NRO 11619.
[9] Dotland Common enclosure award, 1759: NRO 11619.
[10] G Ridley, 'The enclosure and division of certain wastes and commons in the manor of Hexham', *AA*, 5th ser, 2, (1974), p.223.
[11] Northumberland in 1814, by William Anderson of Edinburgh: *Proceedings of the Society of Antiquaries*, 3rd series, Vol 6, (1913-4), p.228.
[12] Estate map of Foggett, 1820: NRO 309/G4/3.
[13] Unpublished English Heritage Management Survey, (2013).
[14] Visitation Report 1805: TNA ADM 79/56.
[15] Visitation Report 1817: TNA ADM 80/59. Other references to the Greenwich Hospital estate in this period draw on this report.
[16] NRO 309/G4/3. Later references to Dotland in this period draw on this document.
[17] 18 Feb 1835: TNA ADM 80/20.
[18] Tithe surveys 1839: NRO DT /243, 245.
[19] D Petts, 'Landscapes of Belief: Non-Conformist Mission in the North Pennines', *International Journal of Historical Archaeology*, 15:3, (2011), pp.461-80.
[20] The Carr/Johnson letters give an illuminating insight into a small Hexhamshire estate of 420 acres under pressure in the late 19th century: NRO 3453.
[21] Estate map NRO 309/G4/3; Clavering estate sale particulars April 1912.
[22] Sale papers for Hesleywell: NRO 3453/4/15.
[23] D Hutt, 'Linnels Mill', North East Mills Group, (2000).
[24] I Hancock, 'Forestry between the Tyne and the Derwent, 1770-1870', *HH*, 28 (2018), p.70. This article gives an excellent overview of the importance of forestry during a century of great change.
[25] J Bailey & G Culley, 1805, quoted in Wm Marshall, *The Review and Abstract of the County Reports to the Board of Agriculture*, (1818), Vol 1, p.47.
[26] The Forestry Commission acquired the land in 1930. Planting started the following year, was completed by 1943, and then extended further after 1957: https://www. forestryengland.uk/ forest-planning/ slaley-forest-plan; E Mason, *A Slaveleia Miscellany*, (new edition as *Slaley, Then and Now*, 2009), p.122.
[27] *Pers comm*, Derek White and Albert Robinson, both now deceased.
[28] NRO CC/CM/SH/10; H Kristensen, *Memories of Hexhamshire*, (1999), p.103.
[29] C Enderby, 'Racing in Hexham', *HH* 27, (2017); NRO ZGI/Do, 9 Aug 1670.

7. Twentieth century connections

Farming revived

As with the French revolutionary and Napoleonic wars of a century earlier, the First World War brought the need to increase domestic food production, because of the disruptions wrought by war to normal patterns of trade. The wartime years did not mark a turning point in the fortunes of local agriculture, although conditions in the post-war period were mild compared to the severity of the depression after 1815. And within the Shire a more interventionist role taken by the state left a new and distinctive feature in the local landscape – the County farms.

Attempts to halt the depopulation of rural England featured among the policies of the Liberal government after 1906. Legislation to encourage smallholdings was passed in 1907 and 1919, with the later Act providing funds to County Councils to buy suitable land where there was demand from ex-servicemen. Northumberland's county council response was rapid and enthusiastic. Among its purchases was 1,870 acres of land in Hexhamshire bought from Wentworth Beaumont, Lord Allendale, in 1919 (see Figure 83). This comprised the Radcliffe land originally forfeited to the Greenwich Hospital in 1735 and sold on by the Hospital to the Beaumont family in 1874.[1] The estate was intended to provide 27 farmholdings, including several new farmhouses. The scheme was beset with problems, not least the distress of existing tenants served with notices by their new Council landlord to quit entirely, or in some cases to lose half of their land. Only 12 of the holdings were let by the end of 1920, each of around 50 acres of generally poor land. Local timber and stone was obtained from the estate's plantations (see above) and quarry. However the contract to build the distinctive eight new farmsteads with steep-pitched roofs such as at Rawgreen, Aydon Shields, Hagwood and Peacock House, was not awarded until later in 1920. Thanks to a combination of poor weather, difficulty in obtaining builders, and shortages of supplies they were not available for occupation until 1922 and 1923. The Council's new tenants often had to find additional work to make a living from their land, yet the rent they paid had still not covered the Council's outgoings and loan interest by the 1950s. This well-intended initiative therefore had decidedly mixed results.[2] But for the sharp recovery of farming fortunes during the Second World War, the outcome might have been worse.

While the First World War had led to a brief revival in farming fortunes, the vulnerability of food supply then was fresh enough in Whitehall's memory for a much more vigorous policy of intervention from

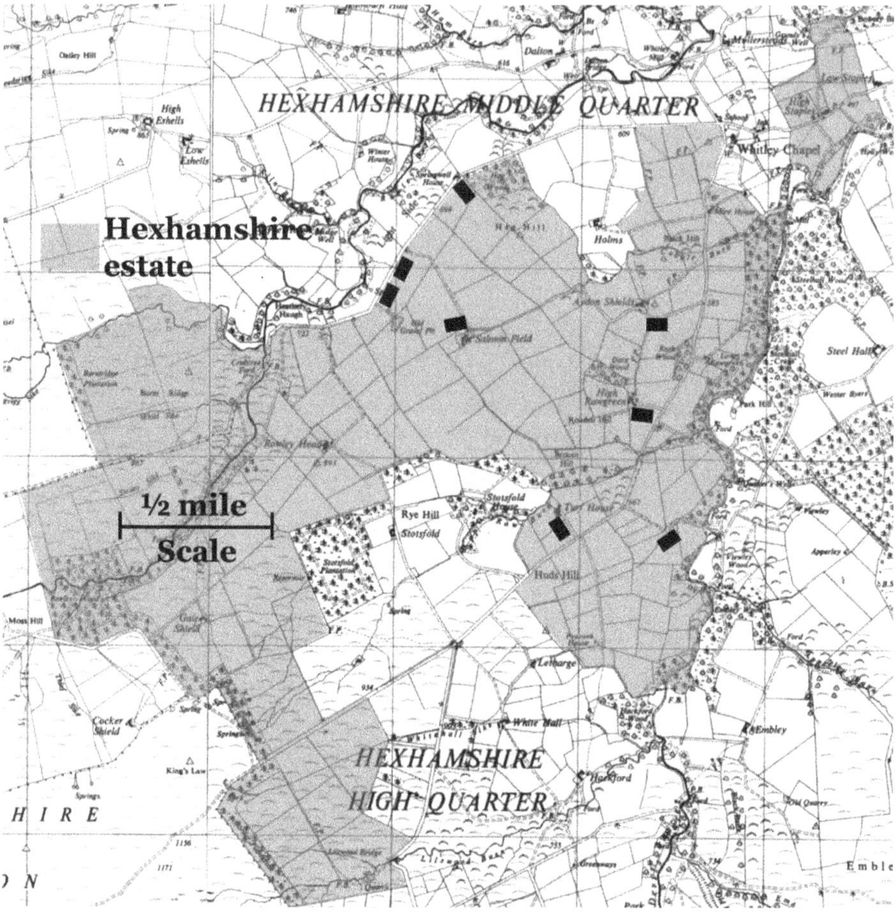

Fig 83: Eight new farmhouses were built for smallholdings by Northumberland County Council in 1921-3 on land bought from the Allendale Estate in 1919. Until 1874 the land had been in the hands of the Greenwich Hospital (OS base 2.5in, 1950).

the start of the Second World War. Once again the tide of arable farming washed up onto the thin upland soils, accompanied by serious mechanisation in the form of tractors. The County War Agricultural Executive Committee was in the driving seat. With food imports once again curtailed, the 'War Ag' had the power to direct what would be sown for crops, based upon comprehensive surveys of the land they undertook in 1940-1. They could – and did – remove farmers from their land if they refused to comply.

The uplands reverted to pasture after the war, but the memory of the vulnerability of imported food in times of crisis drove supportive public policy towards farming and rural areas. Medium-voltage wires carried electricity southwards into the Shire on wooden poles in the 1950s, which assisted the survival of dairying. Wide-span, multi-purpose concrete

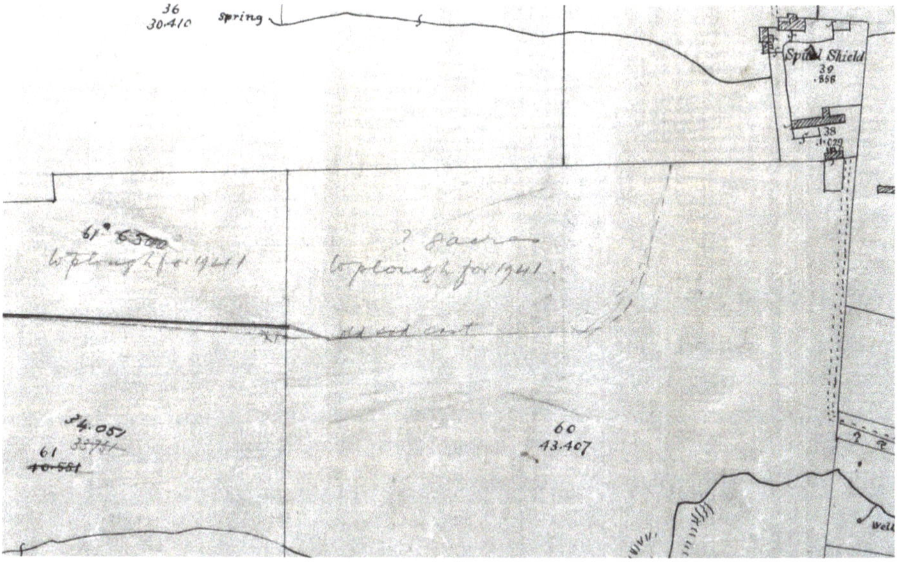

Fig 84 (top): County farm at Aydon Shields, completed and first let in 1923.
Fig 85 (above): Spital Shield, 1940, from a map marked with land to be ploughed in 1941 – at nearly 1,000ft high on the cold clay.

and steel farm sheds were later built for large machinery, to provide winter housing for livestock suitable for meeting modern animal welfare regulations and to economise on scarce farm labour. From the 1980s, stacks of silage bales arrived as a seasonal feature of the modern pastoral landscape. Silage-making had been recognised in principle since the 1880s, reducing the previous vulnerability of haymaking to rainy weather, but it

Fig 86: West Greenridge Farm, with late 20th century sheds and large silage clamp

was only with big bale silage-making and wrapping technology, in which the Shire played an early role, that it became sufficiently less labour-intensive to be widely adopted. The heavy footprint of modern agriculture is often bemoaned, but its adaptation to today's markets and constraints is only the latest in a long history of flexibility and change seen over the millennia. It also signals resilience and survival. Today's new structures are a further contribution to tomorrow's landscape heritage, alongside rigg and furrow, thorn hedges, dry stone walls, post-and-wire fencing, imposing Georgian farmhouses and Victorian byres.

Infrastructure and the landscape

Compared with the decades of sharp decline throughout most of the 19th century the Shire's population was reasonably stable between the 1890s and the Second World War. The first half of the 20th century saw pockets of new building, including the County farms and private developments such as at Juniper. More recently, durable 19th century farm buildings have been converted into housing as the needs and scale of farming has changed. Some of these – and occasional new bungalows – grace individual farmsteads and there have been more substantial developments elsewhere. Ordley was converted in the mid-1980s, Rawgreen at around the same time, and Dotland's extensive yard developed into housing in 1991-2. St Helen's Gate was built at Whitley Chapel to provide council housing in the 1990s. These recent developments are reflected in a reversal since 1981 of several decades of renewed slow population decline in the Shire since World War Two.

Fig 87 (top): Detached and semi-detached housing of the inter-war period in Juniper
Fig 88: Hexhamshire population since 1901

Alongside the modernisation of farming, and a renewal of population growth in new and improved houses, another major trend that has affected life and the local landscape in the century since the First World War, and especially since 1945, has been the extension of many forms of modern infrastructure. Widened tarmac roads accompanied motorised transport.

Fig 89 (top) and 90: Dotland in 1968, a working farm with adjacent Victorian farmyard and cottages behind the 1807 farmhouse built by the Claverings, and in 1991, newly developed for housing

Fig 91: Dukesfield bridge under construction in the 1930s. Telegraph poles alongside the road bring another form of modern communication into the Shire

Several bridges were built where streams had previously only been forded, such as over the Rowley Burn and Ham Burn either side of Dalton crossroads and across the Devil's Water below Dukesfield (see Figure 91). Improvements in physical communications were followed by telephone lines southwards from Hexham (into the northern part of the Shire), and westwards from Slaley. In the fullness of time, public telephone boxes will turn out to have been short-lived roadside adornments at Whitley Chapel and by the Dipton Mill, used less and less as phone lines reached more and more houses. The early 21st century mobile phone mast on Hag Hill between Aydon Shields and the Lightside Road, and the wireless broadband tower above Walley Thorn mark the next wave of mobile telecommunications and high-speed broadband. Wires still sway between poles across the land but digital communication is now largely invisible, aside from receiver dishes on the eaves of many houses.

At the start of the 20th century household water and light relied upon domestic wells, pumps, candles and lamps but as electricity provision became widespread it relied upon centralised generation and distribution through pylons and cables. So too the water supply. From 1889, Hexham's increasing demand for water was met by spring-fed tanks eight miles away at an altitude of 1,300ft (430m) at Ladle Wells, south of Westburnhope, and piped alongside the Rowley Burn. A second pipe was added in 1931, feeding

Figs 92-95: 20th and 21st century infrastructure. Communications provided via roadside telephone lines *(top left)* and mobile phone mast *(top right)*. Electricity carried over pylons *(above left)* and delivered via solar panels. The wireless broadband receiver dish is another 21st century domestic fitting.

a reservoir at Black House corner. A separate reservoir was established at Cocker Shield to supply water to the County farms in the 1920s and was gradually extended to reach other properties.[3] Heating, on the other hand, remains mainly decentralised in the early 21st century and reliant primarily on solid fuel and oil tanks. Although part of the national gas pipeline network was laid across the Shire in the 1970s it does not provide any local supplies. The early 21st century has seen something of a shift back towards decentralisation with the appearance of south-facing solar panels on rooves and in fields, and a few windmills.

The increasing amount of leisure time that has followed generally rising prosperity has also influenced the modern landscape. Previous communal efforts raised chapels, schools and meeting rooms. From 1920 similar local initiative reused a wooden hut from the prisoner-of-war camp above Middle Dukesfield as a parish hall at Whitley Chapel. A purpose built hall followed in the 1930s, and it was in turn extended with additional facilities in the first years of the 21st century. The adjacent sports field, tennis court, cycle track and play area, and the various benches around the Shire are the contributions of a new age of leisure to the existing working landscape. Catering for increasing travel and tourism, a few simple holiday

Fig 96: 21st century landscape adornments by local residents. An avenue of daffodils planted on the footpath alongside the Devil's Water north of Peth Foot.
Fig 97 (below): The stone circle south of Wagtail Wood, which might well both delight and confuse historians in future centuries.

chalets were built here and there in quiet corners of the Shire in the post-Second World War years, and a caravan park established near Broadwell House. Some of the chalets are already falling into decay, joining the remains of structures left from many previous centuries. Bed-and-breakfast accommodation and self-catered outbuilding conversions make their own contributions to meet the demand from those wishing to enjoy the Shire's quiet countryside.

Fig 98 (top): The 'Angel of the Shire' near Barker House, metalwork sculpture by Christopher Hall
Fig 99: Play area and football field next to the Parish Hall

[1] J Taylor, *England's Border County, A History of Northumberland County Council 1889-1989*, (1989); County Council Smallholdings and Allotments Committee: NRO CC/CM/SH/9 (1919-21) and 10 (1921-25). The housebuilding contract was won by Armstrongs of Blaydon, who were bankrupt by the time it ended.
[2] H Kristensen, *Old Hexhamshire*, (2014), p.83; H Pawson, *A Survey of the Agriculture of Northumberland*, (1961) p.154.
[3] D Jennings, *Hexham 1854-1939*, (2005), pp. 95-124. The pipes are mostly buried, and marked by short cast iron posts here and there, but stretches are visible on some moorland stretches. County farm supply: NRO CC/CM/SH/10.

Figs 100 (top) and 101: Heritage and conservation. Recognising the past in the landscape at Dukesfield arches and *(above)* Quaker's Hole, a community wetland conservation project of the early 2000s

8. Landscape change and preservation

Today's Hexhamshire landscape is not the finished result of a cumulative process that added new features through the centuries to reach a modern 'steady state'. Tides of change have washed in and out. Straddling upland and lowland, land use in the Shire was highly sensitive to climatic variation until the early modern period. Upland cultivation, summer pasturing and settlement has come and gone. Woodland was cleared, grew again, was cleared once more and has since been replanted. Throughout the thousands of years of prehistory, life was probably oriented towards the south of the Shire because the upland ridges provided the most obvious human routeways, rising above the dense natural forest cover of the valleys. A tilt to the north possibly came only with the attraction of supplying the Roman military machine along the Tyne corridor and since the last great expansion of settlement in early medieval times. Hexham, invisible over the racecourse ridge, has arguably only been of fundamental importance to the Shire in the last 800 or 900 years of more intensive market integration. Even during that time, the two hundred years of lead traffic from high North Pennine mines through the Shire's smelting mills and onward to the coast used the ridges and largely ignored the town. The long-distance cattle droving tracks deliberately bypassed it. Today we are connected as never before by modern communications, but because tarmac roads, on which the vast majority of modern transport relies, have left the western and southern moorland alone, the Devil's Water valley is now mostly a quiet byway rather than a through-route.

Sometimes the ebb and flow of change has been rapid when seen against the millennia of human life in the Shire. Three hundred years ago the cluster of corn, lead and fulling mills between Black Hall, Dye House and Dukesfield was a dirty, noisy hive of industry beset with heavy horse-borne traffic, in stark contrast to the leafy quiet of today. Within a very small area below Dukesfield Hall there has been a smelting mill, tile works, light railway and saw mill. All were important in their day, exploiting lead, clay and timber for various purposes, but quite independent of each other in their turn. All that remains of the tile works are a few undulations in the field and the vestiges of a track down to the road junction. The light railway route has all but disappeared, so too the saw mill's presence in the riverside woodland. Only the smelting mill arches remain, the oldest of them all.

Keen eyes might spot the shallow remains of many small quarries here and there. One hundred years ago there was a dusty working quarry near the Lightside cottages below Salmonfield bringing out road and

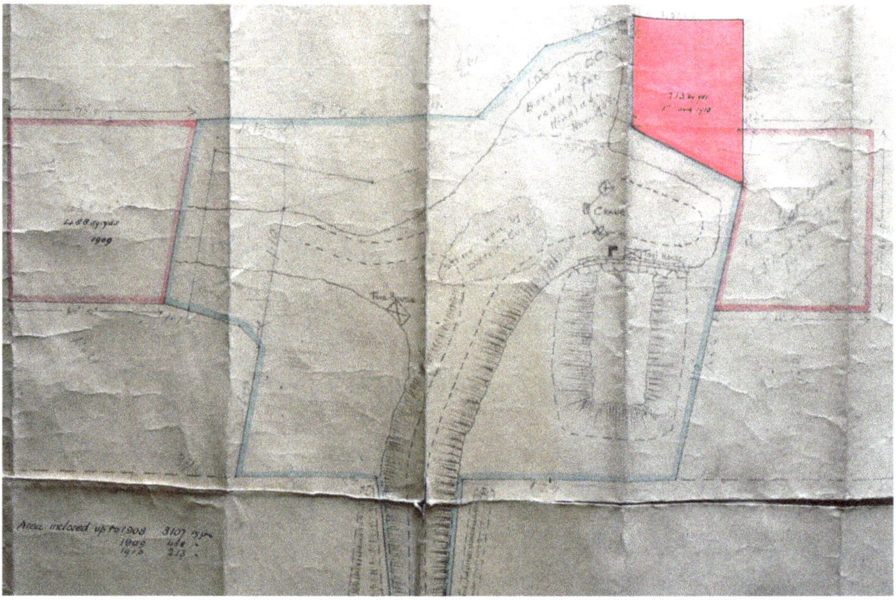

Figs 102 and 103:
Salmonfield Quarry.
The plan above shows the quarry in operation in 1908. Its remains are today fading back into the fields. (Aerial photo: Google Earth)

building stone. Today it too has almost vanished (see Figures 102 and 103). Ephemeral features slip from sight. We only know about Salmonfield's quarry because it was fairly recent and documentary records survive by chance. How many other temporary features have there been which we will never know about?

This gives pause for thought when we consider that the decades since the Second World War are the first in which there has been enough prosperity to give us the choice to preserve entire landscapes for the sake of heritage and aesthetic appeal. Part of the Shire lies within the North

Pennines 'Area of Outstanding Natural Beauty' (although most of that 'natural' beauty is the result of human activity). When statutory planning rules are directed towards limiting development and ensuring it is 'in keeping' with the 'character of the land' we are essentially preserving just the latest remodelling of the land. In the Shire's case this is largely dominated by the great wave of common enclosure since the 1750s. An entire hillside of Iron Age/Romano-British remains was quite possibly swept away by the geometric fields and improvements of the Hexham East common enclosure in the 1750s. Doubtless they were hard on the eye to start with. But who would want their gentle pastoral beauty replaced now (see Figure 104)? The open fells were cleared of woodland by some combination of climatic change and prehistoric agriculture, so in one sense the regimented imported conifers of Slaley Forest and the Fell Plantation have arguably turned their skyline into a closer resemblance of the hills of 6,000 years ago than the adjacent open heather growing on the peat hags. Graceful Georgian houses and solid foursquare farmsteads were once new and garish.

And when faced with choices, what do we decide to preserve, permit and reject? If listed building status is any guide, the 20th century appears to matter less than earlier times. Of the 47 listed buildings in the Shire, 12 date from before about 1700, 14 from the 18th century and 19 from the 19th. Only two 20th century structures are listed – St Helen's church gateposts and a metal milepost.[1] The past century has seen great progress, trauma, prosperity and technical change. Relative labour scarcity alongside an explosion in the applications of metal, concrete and various plastics have

Fig 104: Hexham East Common: the geometric pattern of 18th century Parliamentary enclosure now settled into the modern landscape

Fig 105: Queen's Letch Cottage

led inevitably to the construction of pre-fabricated, standardised farm buildings instead of the locally hand-hewn stone and slate of earlier centuries. The older stone buildings have already demonstrated their durability, but some of the more recent are already decaying, rusting and disappearing. Landscape historians of the future might cherish the fragile and rare survival of the concrete platform of a 1950s milking parlour much as we value the remains of bastle houses.

Walking northwards towards Hexham up the footpath from the Dipton Mill and Hole House, following the Hexham East enclosure hedges, you come across the remains of basic industrial brick walls and associated rubble strewn in a small copse (see Figure 105). This was Queen's Letch Cottage, a simple early to mid-20th century utilitarian dwelling of a family who lived a hard life there without modern utilities until well into the post-war period. Already it is falling back to the earth, another ephemeral feature of the modern landscape. Who is to say it is any less poignant than the older, crumbling stone walls of Winter House or Hall Shield?

As this and future generations apply their wits to new threats and opportunities, and as the climatic pendulum continues to swing, our current landscape will carry on evolving. The current snapshot will be replaced by another. Glimpses of once commonplace features will also continue becoming rare and distant, but still there to add variety to rural views and fuel to the fire of our eternal curiosity.

[1]A further 38 structures listed include 29 18th century boundary stones on the fell, four bridges and five headstones in the graveyard. See https://britishlistedbuildings.co.uk/england/hexhamshire-northumberland#. YcyOiGjP2Uk

Old and new hedging. *Fig 106 (top):* The base of a long-established, horizontally laid hedge near Dotland. *Fig 107:* Grant-assisted new hedging in 2021

Further Reading

The genre of landscape history arguably commenced with W G Hoskins' *The Making of the English Landscape* (1954), stimulating a great deal of later research. The archaeologist Francis Pryor (in 2010) and geographer Nicholas Crane (in 2016) have produced more recent general surveys, both entitled *The Making of the British Landscape*. Two works by Oliver Rackham, *The History of the Countryside* (1986), and *Woodlands* (2010) are excellent guides to reading the historic landscape. Volume 7 of English Heritage's England's Landscape series, *The North East*, (2006), edited by Fred Aalen, is a well-illustrated general survey of the geology, archaeology and history of the region north of the Humber and east of the Pennines.

Robert Newton's *The Northumberland Landscape* (1972) is still helpful in places, and Leslie Hepple's *A History of Northumberland and Newcastle-upon-Tyne* is a concise general history that understandably links the county's history to the strong influence of the economic centre of Newcastle. John Talbot White's *The Scottish Border and Northumberland* (1973) contains a great deal on the county's geology, flora and fauna, which all provide important context for a study of its landscape.

The papers and extended introduction drawn together by Paul Frodsham in *Archaeology in Northumberland National Park* (2004) is very useful and particularly strong on the prehistoric period, as is Waddington and Passmore's *Ancient Northumberland*, also published in 2004. For the early medieval period, Max Adams' *The King in the North* (2013) and *The First Kingdom* (2021), while national in their breadth, have much on the north-east. Richard Lomas, *County of Conflict: Northumberland from Conquest to Civil War* (1996) covers the high medieval period, and Chris Tolan-Smith's *Landscape Archaeology in Tynedale* (1997) has much of local relevance. There are several useful chapters in Faulkner, Berry and Gregory (eds) *Northern Landscape; Representations and Realities of North-East England* (2010), particularly those by Cousins, Purdue and Caunce that make up Part One. The second edition of Pevsner's *The Buildings of England – Northumberland* by Grundy, McCombie, Ryder and Welfare (1992) is a vital work of reference. More recently, Peter Ryder's *Towers and Bastles* (2021) provides a thorough survey of the county's defensible 12th to 16th century smaller buildings.

As far as Hexham and Hexhamshire are directly concerned, Tom Corfe's *Hexham Heritage* (1999) is a very good short introduction to the town's past. While now well over a century old, the three local volumes of the Northumberland County History – 3: A B Hinds, *Hexhamshire Part 1*,

(1896), 4 (in particular): J C Hodgson, *Hexhamshire Part 2*, (1897) and 6: J C Hodgson, *Bywell St Peter, Bywell St Andrew, Slaley*, (1902) – still provide highly useful source information and transcripts of original documents on our area and individual properties within it, even if some of the genealogy is speculative. Stewart Ainsworth's unpublished report 'Shedding Light on the North Pennines, The Allen Valleys and Hexhamshire Lidar Landscape Survey' (2016) is an authoritative summary of the work undertaken as part of the North Pennines Altogether Archaeology project. The report is now available from the website of the project's successor, the community archaeology charity of the same name at https://altogetherarchaeology.org/reports.php. Britnell, Etty and King's edition of *The Black Book of Hexham* (2011) is the first English translation of Hexham Priory's survey of 1379, and has a very useful introduction. It is published by the Hexham Local History Society, whose annual journal *Hexham Historian* contains many articles on the Shire's history. A free cumulative index to the journal is available from the Society's website: https://www.hexhamhistorian.org/product-category/hexham-historian/.

Two books by Hilary Kristensen, *Memories of Hexhamshire*, (1999), and *Old Hexhamshire*, (2014), contain a large number of historic photographs, newspaper extracts and reminiscences from older residents of life in the Hexhamshire landscape. They provide a vital record of key aspects of the Shire's history, and provide particularly vivid snapshots of the late 19th and 20th centuries. For those who wish to explore original material in greater depth, the free online 'Dukesfield Documents' archive contains transcripts of a wide variety of letters and other documents roughly from the mid-17th to mid-19th century loosely centred on the lead industry in the north-east and the land and people around it. The text can be fully searched and as of the summer of 2022 has over 3 million words of content: www.dukesfield.org.uk/documents.

Among the best resources available are the maps of the Ordnance Survey (OS). Old maps at various scales dating from the first edition, surveyed in this region in 1860 (and published in 1865), are available online from the National Library of Scotland (https://maps.nls.uk/). A variety of walks are set out in numerous guide books and websites for those who wish to explore the land for themselves, but footpaths, bridleways and other public rights of way are all clearly marked on the current issue of the 1:25,000 scale OS Explorer Map OL43 'Hadrian's Wall'.

Image acknowledgements

I greatly appreciate the generosity of those who have given permission for their images to be reproduced.

Figures 4, 9, 19, 63: Graham Dixon;
Figures 20, 38, 71, 85, 102: Allendale Estate collection; reproduced by kind permission of Hon Wentworth Beaumont;
Figures 34, 52: Peter Ryder;
Figures 47, 66, 74, 99, 104: Stefan Sobell;
Figure 50: Yvonne Purdy;
Figure 51: Andy Curtis;
Figures 53, 67, 81, 91: Hilary Kristensen, *Memories of Hexhamshire*, (1999);
Figure 56: The Dipton Mill Inn;
Figure 62: Toby Bailey;
Figure 65: Derwent and Sam Gibson;
Figure 103: Google Earth;
Pages 48, Stonehouse; 58, Linnels Bridge; 102, View near Stobby Lee: Steve & Sue Bland
Excerpts from Ordnance Survey maps (Figures 1, 7, 18, 22, 26, 31, 39, 41, 46, 72, 66, 78, 80, 83) are reproduced from the National Library of Scotland's online collection, under respective terms of permissive use.
LiDaR imagery has been generated using Quick Terrain Reader software from the Environment Agency database, 2016. All rights reserved.
All other diagrams, photos and maps, including additions to base Ordnance Survey maps, are by the author, or (Figures 89 and 90) in his collection.

Index

Places in Hexhamshire are accompanied by either a 4 digit or 6 digit National Grid reference shown in *italics*. All are within the Ordnance Survey's NY national grid square. The 4 digit references indicate the southeast corner of a 1km square within which the indexed feature is found; 6 digit references give a more precise point location of the place referred to.

Lightning Source UK Ltd.
Milton Keynes UK
UKHW020647121122
412017UK00003B/8

9 780956 507884